THE FOOTBALL BOOK
FOR KIDS

THE HISTORY OF FOOTBALL, THE GREATEST PLAYERS OF ALL TIME, AMAZING GAMES, AND INCREDIBLE FACTS

LEONARD MATT

TOMOKAI RIVER

CONTENTS

INTRODUCTION

Football has always been a massive part of my life. Born in Nottingham, England and still living there to this day, the city I grew up in has a lot of football history connected to it. For instance, one of the first established football league clubs in the world is claimed to be Notts County, a team founded in Nottingham in 1862.

The city is also home to the closest two football grounds in the UK. On either side of the River Trent, just 270 metres apart, stand the home stadium of Notts County, called 'Meadow Lane' and Nottingham Forest's world famous 'City Ground'.

My first memory of football was Christmas day in 1989. I was four years old and I was looking at my first football, although I didn't know it yet, as it was wrapped in red wrapping paper with Christmas trees all over. I ripped off the paper to reveal a leather sphere covered in red and white hexagons.

A logo on the side of the ball had an outline of a tree with one word: 'Forest'. That one word would change my life forever. Nottingham Forest FC had just become my team. I wanted to know everything about them, their players, where they played football, their manager and any other trivia I could find about them.

I remember not being able to contain my excitement at the thought of playing with my new ball in the garden and that's exactly what I did. I honestly couldn't tell you anything else I got that Christmas. I remember my friend on the same street getting a Sega Master system that year, which is basically the same thing as having a state-of-the-art gaming PC in today's world. I wasn't interested.

All I could think about from then on was football. I remember going to my first match. The experience was something I'll never forget. It was an away match. Chelsea v Nottingham Forest in October of 1990.

It was almost my 5th birthday and my dad, who wasn't a big football fan himself, managed to get tickets from a friend, because he knew I'd been wanting to go since Christmas. We had to get the train to London for a 3 pm kick-off and the train was full of fans chanting and singing, laughing and joking, nervous and excited about the upcoming game.

'What's the score gonna be, mate?' an old man on the train asked me when he noticed I had a red and white scarf around my neck. '4 nil,' I replied confidently. The man smiled and said, 'I hope you're right son!' I'll never forget that conversation, but unfortunately I learned one thing that day: that I'm not a psychic. The game finished goalless. All the build-up and excitement leading up to the match and not a single goal was scored! To me it didn't matter. We came back on the same train with a legion of fans all singing the same song, and I went to school the next day to tell all of my friends about it.

We played football before school, we played at school during lunch times, we played after school and played at weekends.

Nothing could beat the feeling of scoring a wonder goal in front of your friends and performing your favourite player's celebration. I enjoyed pulling my shirt over my head like Fabrizio Ravanelli and running around the pitch with my arms waving with excitement, hoping not to bump into anyone!

Although I loved and still love playing and watching football, I also have a love for history, which is why I decided to combine them to create this book. The book is for anyone already interested in the global phenomenon of world football or anyone new to the sport who wants to learn about it as much as I did all those years ago. I have included fun facts and history of this beautiful game that I have studied over years of watching, playing and writing about the game we in the UK call 'footy'. I hope you enjoy reading this book as much as I have enjoyed writing it.

Thank you for reading.

THE HISTORY OF FOOTBALL

Football, or 'The Beautiful Game', as it is affectionately known by over 4 billion fans all around the world, is the biggest sport in the entire world. It is watched and played on almost every continent, including Europe, South America, Africa and Asia.

You may think of footballers today as global superstars and celebrities with millions of followers on social media, and you may even dream as I did of one day lacing up your boots and walking out onto the fresh green pitch to an army of fans chanting your name as you dazzle them with your flicks and tricks before scoring the winning goal and leaving as a hero!

The life of a professional footballer today comes with plenty of benefits, but it also comes with a lot of hard work and determination. Players today have a rigorous training schedule that involves physical and mental training on top of a strict diet routine to ensure they are performing at the highest possible level. Even lower down in the leagues and as far down as youth level football, players must adhere to a strict regime in order to be scouted ahead of the millions of others who dream of being a professional football player.

Even then, when you train hard through blood, sweat and tears, there is only a small chance you will make it as a professional, and an even smaller chance you will make it as a top professional playing in the best leagues in the world. That said, the feeling of taking the ball swiftly around your opponent with a step-over and then sending the goalkeeper the wrong way with a glance of your head before you guide the ball carefully and precisely into the bottom corner of the goal is a feeling you can't replicate unless you actually play the game.

This means that billions of people worldwide play this sport, not for the money and celebrity status of being a professional player, but for the fun and excitement they get from playing the sport with their friends. The game of football hasn't always been like this, though. Let's take a look at where it all began and how it became the global phenomenon it is today.

WHERE DID THE GAME COME FROM?

The game of association football originated in Britain in the 19th century. But it didn't start there. This book will focus on the modern game of football as we know it today; however, it is important to understand the history of the game and where it all began.

Football, or soccer, as it's known in some parts of the world, has been played in many different forms for a very long time. Even dating back over 2,500 years ago in many different cultures and countries across the world in China, Greece, Rome and the Mesoamerican tribes, such as the Aztecs, some kind of competitive sport has been recorded involving an object being kicked or thrown around in an attempt to claim victory over an opponent.

Some of the earlier forms of football were very dangerous and sometimes involved an entire village, including men, women and even children competing against each other for possession of an inflated pig's bladder! The term 'pigskin' is still used today as a slang term for a football, but thankfully they are now made of leather with a balloon inside made from rubber.

HOW HAS THE GAME EVOLVED OVER TIME?

As time went on, the game of football took many different forms with many different rules being played by different groups of people. Some groups would use their hands while some would have different targets to hit the ball into.

It is believed the Romans were responsible for bringing some kind of ball game to the shores of Britain, where it would later evolve into the game we know today, but there are also claims that the British created their own variant of the game that billions of people now play across the globe.

In the early 19th century, the game in some form was being played in schools and universities, with a number of different rules being played across different schools. The first known set of rules was attempted to be put in place by 'Two old Shrewsbury boys' from Cambridge University, named H. De Winton and J. C. Thring. The pair persuaded a few members of Eton to join them to form a club.

Later on in 1847, Eton College issued another set of rules of their own. Over the next few years, several different sets of rules emerged from various schools and colleges or towns and cities. Most notably were the 'Sheffield Rules' and 'Cambridge Rules', but in 1863 a new set of 'Cambridge Rules' was drawn up by a committee of seven members from former pupils of Eton, Shrewsbury, Harrow, Westminster and Marlborough.

Although a new set of rules was in place, there were still disagreements on how the game should be played, just as there are today. Just as the use of technology in football is constantly evolving -

for example with the advancements of VAR and goal-line technology, which we will cover later on in this chapter - the founders of football were debating different rules that would influence the game still to this day.

Certain members of the founding committee were much more in favour of a 'passing' game that allowed them to pass forward and not worry about being in an offside position. Others wanted to play a more 'dribbling' type of game that had a tight offside rule similar to today's game. If you don't know the offside rule just yet, don't worry, we will cover it in the next chapter.

The Football Association

Commonly known today as the FA, The Football Association is the oldest governing body in football. It was founded way back in 1863 by a London solicitor named Ebenezer Morley. Morley formed Barnes FC in 1862 and is widely considered the 'Father' of The Football Association.

Apparently, Morley wrote a letter that was printed in a popular newspaper called *Bell's Life*, suggesting that there should be a more organised way of playing the game, and proposed a unified set of rules like they already had in the sport of cricket. This led to a historic meeting.

Picture the scene: October 1863 is a very significant year in the history of football, as this is where the game truly began to take shape in an organised fashion, with common rules across all teams involved that are mostly still followed today, with only a few minor tweaks over the years.

Ebenezer Morley met with representatives of other clubs from across England. They gathered in London at The Freemasons' Tavern in Great Queen Street, with a common goal (pardon the pun!) to establish a set of rules and regulations that would be followed by all founding members and anyone who joins the

Association. The aim was to make the game more accessible to both players and spectators in the hope of growing it into something bigger.

The Founding Clubs

There were 11 founding members of The Football Association, which were:

1. Barnes FC
2. Blackheath
3. Blackheath Proprietary School
4. Civil Service
5. Crusaders
6. Forest of Leytonstone (later known as Wanderers FC)
7. No Names Club from Kilburn (Honestly, that was their name!)
8. Crystal Palace (later known as the Royal Engineers AFC)
9. Kensington School
10. Percival House (later known as Blackheath FC)
11. Surbiton

These were the first 11 clubs to play by the standardised rules, which went on to become adopted by teams all over the world in over 200 countries!

EARLY RULES

Field Markings

One of the first rules created by the FA was to create a standard playing field size of up to 180 metres in length and 90 metres in width. There were no markings on the pitch like we see today, just four corner flags marking out the pitch area. Can you imagine being an assistant referee in those days?

It wasn't until 1891 that field markings became a thing. The new pitch included a touch line around the perimeter of the pitch, a goal line 18 yards from the touch line and a penalty line, which was 12 yards from the touch line. It is amazing to think that over 150 years later, the goal area and penalty kick distance have not changed at all. It was 12 yards then and it's 12 yards today.

The difference with penalty kicks in 1891 was that the player had the option to place the ball anywhere across the dotted 12-yard line, as opposed to today, where players stand directly in front of the goalkeeper and must place the ball on the penalty spot.

In 1902, a new pitch was created, which looks almost identical to the pitch we see today. The only differences are the semi-circles on the edge of the 18-yard box and the quarter-circles in each corner, within which players must stay when placing a ball down for a corner kick.

The FA Cup

The FA is also responsible for the oldest football competition in the world.

In 1871, the FA created The Football Association Challenge Cup. Today, you might hear this called the FA Cup, or if you are reading this in the UK, just 'the Cup.' It has been won by some of the biggest teams in England and is also one of the only chances a small team from the lower leagues has to play one of the bigger teams.

When a smaller team is drawn up against a top tier team, there is a certain magic about the FA Cup that can bring out the best in any player of any team. In fact, it's not uncommon for these lower league - or sometimes even non-league teams - to claim victory over their somewhat mightier opponents in what is known across the footballing world as a 'Giant Killing.'

The first FA Cup match was played between Wanderers and Royal Engineers, both founding clubs of the Association. The match was held at the Kennington Oval in front of about 2,000 spectators. Compared to the prices of today's tickets, you could have seen this historical fixture of tournament football for just one shilling (today, 20 shillings is equivalent to one pound)!

It was Wanderers who came out victorious, but only just. The game ended with one goal separating the two teams, which was scored by Wanderers' striker Morton Betts. Wanderers' success didn't end there, though; they went on to win five consecutive FA Cup trophies in the following years!

What separates the modern era from historical football?

As well as the price of the tickets, much has changed on and off the pitch since the 19th century. The game has rapidly spread to over 200 countries, from Britain to Argentina, Brazil, Spain, Germany, Nigeria, and South Korea. Some of the most remote parts of the world have football teams registered with The Football Association. Even Lapland, yes Lapland, have their own football team, and it's called FC Santa Claus! Look it up if you don't believe me. They were founded in 1992 and play their football in the fifth tier of the Finnish football league.

When the game turned professional in 1885, only a handful of players were paid to play. The first player recorded as being transferred to another club was Willie Groves. He transferred from West Bromwich Albion to Aston Villa for 100 pounds and he was paid four pounds per week. Compare that to today's players, who transfer between clubs for eye-watering sums of money, some upward of 100 million pounds! At first, the FA were against the idea of paying players to play, and it wasn't until the early 20th century that it became more accepted.

Today, football is a multi-billion pound industry with huge investment from sponsors, millions of shirt sales every year and some of the most iconic and legendary stadiums ever built.

Technology in football

As technology advanced to the present day, football advanced with it, at an astounding rate. I don't think even Ebenezer Morley could have quite visualised the progression of his initial idea to organise the game for the benefit of the billions of players and fans. We now have technology such as Video Assistant Referee (VAR), which gives the referee the chance to watch back any close calls or challenging decisions on a screen at the side of the pitch. They can now choose to slow down the action and even rotate the camera angle, as well as use imaginary lines to get offside decisions right almost every time. Referees today also have the help of Goal Line Technology, which is a laser beam that shoots across the goal line. If the ball touches the laser beam, it triggers a vibration in the ref's watch around his wrist, and they know that the goal should be given. The equipment is supplied to the top levels of the sport by the Hawk-Eye company, which has a control room set up with monitors watching the game at all different camera angles.

The first match to use VAR was on the first of September 2016 between France and Italy. It was a friendly match with the purpose of testing the VAR system for use in the future and it didn't take long before there was a need for assistance when it came to game-changing decisions. In just the 4th minute, the referee, Björn Kuipers, was faced with a possible red card situation. Djibril Sidibé of France had fouled Daniele De Rossi of Italy, and some Italian players protested for a red card. Through an earpiece from the Hawk-Eye assistant, Kuipers heard a voice in his ear telling him there was no need for him to issue the red card and a more suitable punishment of a yellow card was given instead.

Before this technology, it was down to the eagle eye of the referee alone to decide whether it was, in fact, a goal or not. Hundreds of controversial decisions over the years could have been avoided entirely with the luxury of an instant replay in real-time for the referee. If VAR was available in the 1976 World Cup, Diego Maradona wouldn't have gotten away with his incredible 'Hand of God' goal that put Argentina into the final! Prior to the introduction of assisted technology in football, the final decision of any dispute was ultimately decided by the referee based on what he saw in real-time.

Cultural changes

For many years, the world of football was typically seen as a 'man's game.' Even when I was at school in P.E. class, the boys would play football or rugby while the girls would play netball or hockey. There were always girls who liked football as much as the boys did, but they never got the chance to play at a team level, beyond just having a kick around with their friends. In recent years, though, there has been a big push to create a path for girls who love football to be able to play at all levels. The women's game has evolved and spread to many parts of the world. The very first Women's World Cup was set up in 1970 and held in Italy, and during the 1970s many countries that had banned women's football started to allow it.

In 2022, England's Lionesses won the Women's World Cup with a 2-1 victory over Germany. Their victory inspired many girls in schools across the country to take part in more football-related activities. Women's football has rapidly advanced to catch up with the men's game in many technological aspects, as well, and is now watched by millions of fans all over the world. There are thousands more clubs and football teams set up for girls to enjoy playing football together with the chance of one day playing at places like Bernabéu or Wembley Stadium! That would likely be surprising for those watching a football match back in the early

19th century, but thankfully football has a great way of bringing all people together.

Tactics

There are plenty of other differences between then and now. If you look at the football that is played tactically today, you will notice a huge difference. I can remember seeing old footage of historic football matches when I was a child. I couldn't understand why everyone on the pitch was just chasing the ball around in a big huddle! Later on, teams began to develop formations. A formation is the set of positions that the team play on the pitch. There are three main areas of the pitch, not including the goalkeepers area. They are defence, midfield and attack. Early on in the development of formations, most teams used to play in a 2-3-5, which meant two fullbacks (defenders), three halfbacks (midfielders) and five forward players (attackers). This developed over the years into a more balanced 4-4-2, with four defenders, four midfielders and two attackers. The 4-4-2 formation is still used today but there is now a much bigger variety of formations used across all leagues. Players today are capable of fluidly switching between positions from defence to attack or attacking midfield to defence.

2

HOW 'THE BEAUTIFUL GAME' IS PLAYED

The rules of football are always changing. Here is how we play the game today. Each team has 11 players on the field at any one time, with the aim of scoring a goal in the opponents' goal net. The team with the most goals after 90 minutes of play, wins. The game is divided into two halves of 45 minutes each, and at half time, the players have a 15 minute break and return to the pitch having changed ends so they are scoring in the opposite goal from the first half.

Managers can bring on up to five substitutions during the game at any time. A substitution is when a player is swapped for another, usually later on in the game, when a player on the pitch is showing signs of tiredness or injury, and sometimes if a manager wants to change tactics or formation during a match. Managers decide who is substituted and when it happens, and sometimes bringing a substitute on in the later stages of a match can have extremely positive outcomes. When a defender is tired and being approached by a skilful winger sprinting down the right wing with full energy, the defender finds it difficult to chase the ball when it is played through for the attacker.

Below is a description of each position and what it means to play there.

Goalkeeper (GK)

The goalkeeper is the last line of defence and the only player on the pitch allowed to use their hands. Their job is to stay within the 18-yard box marked around each end of the pitch and stop the other team from scoring in their goal. They wear special gloves to protect their hands and usually wear a long-sleeved shirt instead of the standard short-sleeved shirt that the players wear. Goalkeepers are usually tall and agile so they can dive across the goal and reach down into the corners to save a precise shot coming at speed.

Defenders

Defenders are responsible for protecting the goalkeeper from having to make saves by trying to take the ball from the attackers of the other team. Unlike goalkeepers, though, they can't use their hands and must use their feet to tackle opponents and use their bodies to block shots. Defenders used to be strong and sturdy members of the team who were tough and not scared of going in for a hard tackle or two. In the modern game, however, a defender comes in all forms, including centre-backs, fullbacks and wingbacks.

Centre-backs (CB)

Centre-backs are strong on their feet and able to pressure attackers into making a mistake. The centre-back in the modern game also has to have speed, because attackers can burst past them at incredible speeds to receive a pass from midfield. They usually stay back when the team is attacking, so if the opponents get the ball and 'counter attack' they can make sure they don't leave themselves open.

Fullbacks (LB, RB)

A fullback is a player who plays on either the right or the left of the pitch in a defensive position. They are normally known as right backs (RB) and left backs (LB). They usually stay around the defensive area and feed the ball to a midfielder or a winger to carry on the attack. Fullbacks used to stay back and defend a lot more than they do now. Players in this position can sometimes overlap the winger and go on a run themselves with the ball down the side of the pitch. This confuses the opposing defenders and allows the winger to move into place inside the penalty area to receive a pass.

Wingbacks (LWB, RWB)

In the modern game, an increasing number of wingbacks are emerging. They play more of an attacking role than a fullback and overlap with the winger more often. They rely on speed over strength and dribbling over defensive knowhow, but a world-class wingback is one who can master all skills. Sometimes full-backs will play as a wingback if that's what the manager wants them to do.

Midfielders

Defensive Midfielder (CDM)

This is also a position that has seen more use in recent years. The defensive midfielder, or CDM, is a strong versatile player who is sometimes referred to as the 'anchor' of the team. They take the ball from defence and distribute it to the rest of the midfield. They usually stay back when attacking and make sure to hold up the play to allow other players to return to their positions. CDMs are players who can be counted on to keep their team in control of the game in midfield. It is said that midfield is usually where the battle is won and lost in football. Control midfield and you will manage the game better and create more attacking chances.

Central Midfielder (CM)

This position is sometimes referred to as box-to-box midfielders because of their ability to not only get back and defend when needed, but also to take the ball into attacking positions. Central midfielders need to be extremely fit to be able to do this for 90 minutes. They need to be agile and quick and have a keen eye for a good pass. They are responsible for controlling the tempo of the game and must chase the ball and win it back if they lose it. This is a key position, and needs a versatile player who can play both defence and attack to a high standard.

Left or Right Midfielders (LM, RM)

Playing on either side of the pitch to allow teams to play with width by passing and dribbling the ball up the pitch from the flanks is a common way to set up an attack. Usually receiving a pass from the fullbacks, or offering a passing option for a central midfielder, LMs and RMs need to be fast and fit to last for the entire match as they run up and down either side with the ball on an attack, or without the ball, chasing the attacker to win back possession. Dribbling is an important part of a LM or RM's game, as is a good crossing technique, which refers to whipping the ball into the box for an attacker to get onto the end of with either a head or foot/leg.

Attacking Midfielders (CAM)

Although in the midfield category, the attacking midfielder, in case you haven't already guessed, is a midfielder that plays more of an attacking role than a typical CM. When the ball is in the possession of their opponents, an attacking midfielder will be more likely to stay up the pitch with the attackers, or just behind them, waiting for possession to change hands so they can start a counter attack. They have an ability to dribble like a midfielder but have a shot more like a striker, sometimes being able to score amazing goals from outside the box.

Attackers

Wingers (LW, RW)

When picking a formation, managers will usually make a choice between having right and left midfielders, or wingers. When wingers are used instead, they play much further up the pitch in an attacking role rather than the middle of the pitch like a midfielder would. They usually accompany one central attacker, or 'striker' as they are most commonly known, whereas playing LM or RM gives more room to play two central strikers. A good winger has an explosive run and is able to get into place and get the ball into the box, and also has a good enough shot themselves to go on and score without the assistance of a striker.

Strikers (ST)

This position is one that gets the most chances at a goal. It's also the one every aspiring young boy or girl wants to be in the beginning ... well, at least in my case. The striker scores the goals and gets the glory but if they don't score for a few games, they can quickly become a club villain. In today's game, teams will most often opt for either one central striker, or will play without the two wingers and have two strikers up front. Strikers today have the ability to dribble, shoot and sprint quickly for the ball when the midfield picks out a pass for them. Teams usually have to pay the most for strikers because of the number of goals they score.

Centre Forward (CF)

A centre forward is played slightly ahead of the striker and their job is to receive a pass from further back and hold up the ball until players around them can get into an attacking position. They have a crucial role in modern day formations, with two attackers as the centre forward, and are usually taller and stronger than the striker, who is normally the quicker, more agile of the two positions. Both types of attackers are capable of scoring many goals, as they don't need to focus as much on defending; however, the centre forward's ability to shield the ball from defenders makes them a key addition to any squad.

3

THE GREATEST OF ALL TIME

This is the place in the book that the child version of me would have skipped straight to, had I been given this book as a gift. If that's also you, when you have read this section, go back and read the rest of the book at least once! This section, however, would have been re-read and analysed countless times by me as a youngster. I wanted to learn every last detail about the players we consider to be the greatest of all time, or GOAT, for short. No, not that kind of goat! When goats are mentioned in the sporting world, we are not talking about farm animals, we are referring to the best players to have ever played the game - The Greatest of All Time.

We're going to take a look at the best player in every position of the pitch, starting with the goalkeeper and ending with the attackers. We will look at their stats and at what makes them the best of the best. Can you notice any common themes between these players? Think about what makes a player the best as you read this and if professional football is your dream, then getting inside the head of a GOAT may give you some ideas about how to improve your own game on the pitch.

PETER SCHMEICHEL

Full Name: Peter Boleslaw Schmeichel

Nickname: The Great Dane

Born: November 18, 1963

Hometown: Gladsaxe, Denmark

Height: 6'3"

Position: Goalkeeper

National Team: Denmark

Years Playing: 1981-2003

Club Teams: Hvidovre, Brondby, Manchester United, Sporting Lisbon, Aston Villa, Manchester City

Notable Quote: "I'm a goalkeeper, so I'm used to stress."

Peter Schmeichel is known as one of the greatest goalkeepers of all time. Born in Denmark in 1963, Schmeichel began playing football at a young age, but he wasn't always a goalkeeper. He actually started life as a striker and a midfielder, and then switched to the goalkeeper position years later. It was then that his career really started to go places, as Peter's height and agility made him a perfect fit for the position, and he quickly established himself as one of the best goalkeepers in Denmark.

Schmeichel's first big break was in 1981, when he signed with Hvidovre, a Danish club. In the 1985/86 season, it wasn't only his goalkeeping that got people's attention. That season, he managed to score six goals at the other end of the pitch! Six goals in 28 appearances! He went on to score 11 goals in his career, which is very rare for a goalkeeper whose job is to protect their own goal. Most of Schmeichel's goals would come from corner kicks. If his team was losing and there was not much time left in the game, he would leave his goal and get inside the opponent's penalty area if his team won a corner. His huge presence in the box meant he could tower over defenders and head the ball into the net, sometimes getting his team the victory. He would go on to play for several other clubs, including Brondby in Denmark, where he won three league titles, before heading to the shores of England.

He was signed to Manchester United in 1991 by Sir Alex Ferguson for just over half a million pounds, and while that may be a lot of money to us, in modern football, even back then, it was considered cheap for a player of Peter's quality. Even Ferguson, who was manager, said at the time that it was the "bargain of the century"! He wasn't wrong about that either, because Schmeichel helped his team win five Premier League titles, a UEFA Champions League title and three FA Cups. Schmeichel will always be remembered by United fans and neutral football fans across the world for his acrobatics at both ends of the pitch. He even once scored an overhead kick in the last few minutes of a match, although unfortunately for him it didn't count. In 1997, Manchester United played Wimbledon in the FA Cup. The ball was played in from a corner kick and headed towards Schmeichel, who jumped in the air in almost a backflip and kicked the ball into the back of the net past the astounded goalkeeper. The assistant referee's flag went up and the goal was ruled offside. Watching it back on replay, it was clearly the correct decision. Nevertheless, it was an amazing goal that you should check out if you haven't seen it.

Peter made 398 appearances for Manchester United from 1991 to 1999 and in his last season with that club, went out with a bang by helping his team to win what is known as 'the treble.' This is the term used when a team wins the Premier League, The Champions League and The FA Cup. After an outstanding career with Manchester United, Schmeichel went on to play for three more clubs, including Sporting Lisbon, Aston Villa, and United's local rival Manchester City.

Schmeichel's list of career highlights is enough to impress anyone. In addition to his club success, he also played a huge part in the Danish national team during the 90's, helping them to famously win the UEFA European Championship in 1992 for the first time in the country's history. Peter kept a 'clean sheet' (meaning the other team was prevented from scoring) in the final, beating Germany 2-0. He also helped them to win the FIFA Confederations Cup in 1995. After retiring in 2003, Schmeichel remained involved in football. You may even have seen him on your TV as a commentator and pundit, usually for games involving Manchester United and Denmark. The Great Dane's impact on the game of football is still felt today, and he will always be remembered as one of the most talented and successful goal-keepers in the history of the game.

Career Highlights: Five-time Danish Player of the Year, Five-time Premier League Champion, Three-time FA Cup Winner, One-time UEFA Champions League Winner, One-time UEFA European Championship Winner, One-time FIFA Confederations Cup Winner, Inducted into the English Football Hall of Fame.

PAOLO MALDINI

Full Name: Paolo Cesare Maldini

Nickname: Il Capitano

Born: June 26, 1968

Hometown: Milan, Italy

Current City: Milan, Italy

Height: 6'1"

Position: Defender

Years Playing: 1985-2009

Club Team: AC Milan

Notable Quote: "Playing for AC Milan is like being in a religion. We have a lot of expectations, we have to work hard every day and we have to win."

Paolo Maldini is one of the greatest defenders in the history of football. Born in Milan, Italy, Paolo grew up in a very sporting family, so it was almost his destiny to become one of the all-time footballing greats. His father, Cesare Maldini, was also a legendary footballer who played for AC Milan and the Italian national team. As a child, Maldini became obsessed with football; he used to go with his dad to training sessions, and would watch him and the other players practice. From a young age, Paolo was an exceptional athlete and excelled in many sports, such as swimming and tennis. In the end, though, it was football that stole his heart. Paolo always knew that he wanted to be a professional footballer and follow in his dad's footsteps. He joined AC Milan's youth academy at just 10 years old, and quickly stood out as a star player among his teammates.

At the age of 16, Paolo made his debut for AC Milan, the team his father had played for. It was 1985 and it was the start of something special. He was known by anyone who watched him for his composure on the ball, making the game look effortless, and was a nightmare for attackers who had to face him. Maldini was one of those players who was always at the right place at the right time, as if he had a sixth sense for where the ball was going to be. With his leadership skills and presence in the dressing room, he also became the captain of the team at the young age of 22, and wasn't challenged for that position for the rest of his career.

Maldini played as a centre-back but could have also been on this list as a left back, as his ability to perform both roles well makes him easily one of the best defenders the world has ever seen. He played in a total of 902 matches for AC Milan, and he won many trophies that he will always be adored for, including seven Serie A titles, five UEFA Champions League titles, and one FIFA Club World Cup.

Maldini also made 126 appearances for the Italian national team. He played in four World Cups, which is held only once every four years, and helped Italy win the World Cup trophy in 2006. He was known for his loyalty and dedication to his team and was never afraid to go in for a tough tackle. He had perfect timing, and he always gave 100 percent dedication on the pitch.

One of Maldini's most memorable moments, which I remember well, came in the 2005 Champions League final against Liverpool. The game took place in Istanbul, Turkey and by the end of the first half, AC Milan had taken a 3-0 lead, with Maldini himself opening the scoring in the first minute of the game by volleying home a free kick taken by Andrea Pirlo. Crespo went on to score two more goals in the first half, putting AC Milan 3-0 ahead after 45 minutes. After the halftime team talk, Liverpool found some kind of magic and came back to draw the game 3-3 after 90 minutes. The extra time that followed was one of Paolo Maldini's finest performances, as he was able to keep his cool under immense pressure and even put in a crucial block to deny Liverpool scoring a late winner. Unfortunately, it wasn't enough to stop the opposition, and Liverpool went on to win the game on penalties.

Paolo Maldini retired from football in 2009, but remained involved in the sport and, like Schmeichel, went on to become a pundit of TV and, most notable, the sporting director of AC Milan. His love of sport in general even drew him into professional tennis, and in 2018 he played in a doubles match at an ATP (Association of Tennis Professionals) event in Milan.

Paolo Maldini will always be remembered as one of the greatest footballers of all time. He was a true legend of AC Milan and Italian football, and his influence on the sport will be felt for generations to come.

Career Highlights: Seven-time Serie A Champion, Five-time UEFA Champions League Winner, Five-time Supercoppa Italiana Winner, One-time Coppa Italia Winner, One-time UEFA Super Cup Winner, One-time Intercontinental Cup Winner, Inducted into the Italian Football Hall of Fame, Inducted into the UEFA Champions League Hall of Fame.

WENDIE RENARD

Full Name: Wendie Thérèse Renard

Born: July 20, 1990

Hometown: Martinique, France

Position: Centre-back

Club Team: Olympique Lyonnais Féminin #3

National Team: France

Noteable Quote: "You only get one shot and you've got to take it. Even if you're dominated in a match, if you have one chance, you have to know how to go for it. Efficiency is the golden word for me. Every match is just as important, whether it be a final or a league game, and the ambition is always to win."

Wendie Renard is one of the most talented and powerful defenders in women's football today. Born on the Caribbean island of Martinique, Wendie is the youngest of four daughters. She always knew she had a special talent for football. She started playing for her local club, CS Case-Pilote, and it wasn't long before she was being scouted by bigger clubs in her home country of France. At the age of 15 she went to mainland France for a trial with French club Clairefontaine but was not accepted into the national training program. She soon had another trial with Olympique Lyonnais, and by 16 had permanently moved to Lyon to pursue her career. I'm guessing the scout in charge at Clairefontaine is kicking himself now.

Their loss was Lyon's gain, as Renard joined Olympique Lyonnais Féminin (OL) in 2006. She was quickly recognised as a key member of the team and helped OL win a record 14 league titles in a row from 2006 to 2020. She also played her part in a massive eight European Cup wins and seven French Cup wins for her club! One of her proudest moments as a player for OL was her match against Turbine Potsdam of Germany in 2011. This wasn't just any old game for Wendie. It was the final of the 2010/11 UEFA Women's Champions League: one of the most prestigious trophies any player can win. Wendie scored the opening goal of the game that ended 2-0 and allowed her to lift the trophy once again for her side. Renard is known for her height (6'1"), strength, and is famous for her amazing free kicks. In fact, she has scored over 100 goals in her career, many with her head, which is normally unheard of for a defender.

But it's not just her club career that's worth a mention here. Wendie has had an outstanding international career with France, too. She played her first match for France in 2011, and in 2019 she helped them reach the quarter finals of the World Cup. She has also represented France at the Olympics. Renard's success on the pitch has earned her many individual awards and honors. She has been named the French Player of the Year on many occasions and has been included in the FIFPro Women's World XI several times. In 2020, she was named the UEFA Women's Player of the Year, proving her status as one of the best female footballers to ever play the game.

Off the pitch, she also shows tremendous commitment to her community, giving back to charity and helping to raise money for many different charitable organisations. She has even started her own foundation, which aims to promote education and sports for children in Martinique.

Renard has set a standard for defenders in women's football that is hard to match. She has proven that women's football can be just as exciting and competitive as the men's game. Her dedication and passion for the sport are an inspiration to young girls and women around the world, encouraging them to pursue their goals and follow their dreams.

Career Highlights: Ten-time Division 1 Féminine Champion, Seven-time UEFA Women's Champions League Winner, Six-time Coupe de France Féminine Winner, Four-time Trophee des Championnes Winner, One-time SheBelieves Cup Winner, One-time FIFA Women's World Cup Runner-up, One-time Olympic Games Bronze Medalist, Inducted into the French Football Hall of Fame.

CAFU

Full Name: Marcos Evangelista de Morais

Nickname: Cafu

Born: June 7, 1970

Hometown: São Paulo, Brazil

Position: Right back

Height: 5'9"

Club Teams: Retired (Formerly AS Roma, AC Milan, and Brazil national team)

Notable Quote: "Success in football comes from hard work and dedication."

When it comes to football, Cafu is one of the greatest defenders of all time. But did you know that his full name is Marcos Evangelista de Morais? Don't worry, we'll just stick to calling him Cafu.

Just like the previous GOATs mentioned, Cafu also had a passion for football from an early age, He was raised in São Paulo, Brazil, where he played with his friends day and night, but, like most young players, he had to work really hard to be noticed. He had to compete with other talented players to have his chance to play in the big leagues, and coming from Brazil, there was no shortage of young, talented players. Brazil is the most successful international team of all time, winning the World Cup an astonishing five times! Although it has been more than 20 years since they won the tournament, they picked up the title of world champions of football all the way back in 1958. They have won another four World Cups since, in 1962, 1970, 1994 and 2002, with Cafu on the team for both the 1994 and 2002 victories. He is the only player in history to have played in three consecutive World Cup Finals and could have made it three consecutive victories if Brazil had gone on to beat France in the 1998 final in Paris. It wasn't to be, though, as France dominated the game and were declared 3-nil victors.

Cafu's success took a lot of hard work and determination before he made it to the professional level. He played for some of the biggest teams in the world, including AS Roma and AC Milan. His success on the field made him a legend in the world of football. Cafu's skills on the ball were second to none. He was known for his speed down the wing and his ability to play both attack and defence equally. As a right back, he was always in the right position to make a tackle or intercept a pass. His work ethic was also noted by many professionals as one of the best they have ever seen. He trained hard every day of the week to make sure he was always in top form for games. But Cafu wasn't just a great player on the pitch. He was also a leader off it, as well. He was always willing to help his teammates and give them advice.

Now retired, Cafu still remains a legend in the sport and will be remembered by not only Brazillian fans but fans of football around the world. In recent years he has taken to TV commentating, which allows him to share his knowledge and love for football with a wider audience. And who knows, maybe one day we'll see Cafu coaching a team and leading them to victory, just like he did on the field.

Career Highlights: Two-time FIFA World Cup Winner, Two-time Copa America Winner, Two-time UEFA Champions League Winner, Two-time Serie A Winner, One-time UEFA Cup Winner, One-time UEFA Super Cup Winner, One-time Supercoppa Italiana Winner, Inducted into the Brazilian Football Museum Hall of Fame, Inducted into the Italian Football Hall of Fame, Inducted into the UEFA Champions League Hall of Fame.

ASHLEY COLE

Full Name: Ashley Cole

Born: December 20, 1980

Hometown: Stepney, London, England

Height: 5'9"

Position: Left back

Club Teams: Arsenal, Chelsea, Roma, LA Galaxy

Notable Quote: "I'm never satisfied with what I've done. I always want to do more."

Ashley Cole is one of the greatest left backs of all time. He was born in Stepney, London in 1980 and grew up playing football with his friends. As a young boy, he dreamed of playing for his favourite team, Arsenal. He would soon realise his dreams would come true! Cole was a very talented youngster and joined Arsenal's youth academy when he was just nine years old. He worked hard and trained every day to improve his skills, and his efforts paid off when he made his professional debut for Arsenal at the age of 18.

In his first season with the Gunners, Cole showed that he was one of the best left backs in the Premier League. He was fast, strong, and had excellent defensive skills. His speed allowed him to make quick runs down the left hand side of the pitch, often bursting past opponents and leaving them in the dust. He also had great strength, which helped him win the ball back from opposing players.

During his time at Arsenal, Cole won lots of trophies for his childhood team, including two Premier League titles and three FA

Cups. He was also a part of the famous Arsenal "Invincibles" team, which went unbeaten for an entire Premier League season in 2003-04. They were actually unbeaten for longer than that when you consider the previous season. In total, they racked up an impressive 49 games without losing. They were all set to make it 50 when their dreams were brought to an end with a 2-0 defeat to Manchester United. In 2006, Cole made a controversial move to Chelsea, which is considered Arsenals local rival. This left a few Arsenal fans unhappy with him. This happens in football, though, and it was Ashley's ambition to keep playing at the top level that helped him through a difficult time with his former fans.

At Chelsea, Cole continued to be a dominant force up and down the left flank. He helped the team win many trophies, including one Premier League title, four FA Cups, and one UEFA Champions League title. He was also named the Chelsea Player of the Year in 2011. In 2014, Cole made the move to Italian club AS Roma, where he played for two seasons. He then moved to the United States to play for the LA Galaxy in Major League Soccer, or the MLS, for short.

Throughout his career, Cole was known for his excellent defensive skills, his speed and athleticism, and his ability to create scoring opportunities for his teammates. He was also a leader on and off the field, and was respected by his teammates and opponents alike. But more than that, he was a true professional himself, always working hard and striving for excellence. His determination, talent, and leadership will be remembered by football fans around the world for years to come.

Even though Ashley cole is considered one of the best in the world, he was never satisfied with how good he was and was always looking for ways to improve his game and help his team win. Off the field, Cole has been involved in many charitable organisations. He has worked with UNICEF and other groups to help children in need, and has used his platform as a professional athlete to raise awareness for important causes.

Career Highlights: Three-time Premier League Champion, Seven-time FA Cup Winner, One-time UEFA Champions League Winner, 2010 England Player of the Year, 2011 Chelsea Player of the Year.

CLAUDE MAKÉLÉLÉ

Full Name: Claude Makélélé Sinda

Nickname: The Water Carrier

Born: February 18, 1973

Hometown: Kinshasa, Zaire (now the Democratic Republic of Congo)

Height: 5'7"

Position: Defensive Midfielder

Club Teams: Nantes, Marseille, Celta Vigo, Real Madrid and Chelsea

Notable Quote: "I try to do my best for the team, whether it's playing defensively or offensively."

Claude Makélélé is one of the most famous defensive midfielders of all time. In fact, the defensive midfield role was pretty much invented by Makélélé and is now sometimes known as the "Makélélé Role", which refers to a holding midfielder who sits in front of the defence and breaks up the other teams attacks. His nickname is the "The Water Carrier" because of his hardworking play style and his ability to carry his team to victory even when the odds were against them. But his journey to becoming one of the best in the world was not easy.

Makélélé was born in Zaire (now the Democratic Republic of Congo) in 1973, but he moved to France when he was just four years old. Claude faced many challenges on his journey to football excellence, including a language barrier and financial struggles. But football was always his escape and he saw it as a way out of poverty for himself and his family. He would spend hours practising with his friends at school and on the playground. He would practise kicking a ball against the wall for hours to improve his passing technique and spent hours watching games on TV and studying the greats.

Claude knew that if he worked hard and perfected his game, he could achieve great things, but he found it hard at first to live and play away from his family when he was playing in Brittany at just 15 years old. All the hard work paid off when he joined FC Nantes' youth academy at the age of 18. He quickly made his way up to the first team and racked up 169 appearances for his first club and even took them to a UEFA Champions League semi-final in 1995 before making the move to Olympique de Marseille in '97 and then to Spain to play for Celta Vigo in 1998.

But it was at Real Madrid where Makélélé truly made a name for himself in the world of football. Playing for the team for just three years, from 2000 to 2003, he helped them win two Spanish La Liga championships, the Champions League, the Supercopa de España, the UEFA Super Cup and the Intercontinental Cup. And all those hours kicking a ball against a wall meant that Makélélé was also a great passer and could initiate attacks with his accurate long balls. He played with incredible passion and determination, and was always there to give advice to his teammates.

After leaving Real Madrid, Makélélé continued his successful career in the English Premier League (EPL), brought to Chelsea by manager Claudio Ranieri in 2003. He played for Chelsea until 2008 and helped the team win two Premier League titles and the FA Cup during his time there. Makélélé then joined French giants Paris Saint-Germain until he retired from professional football in 2011, but his impact on the sport is still felt today. He was known for his work ethic on the pitch, and his commitment to the team. He was not flashy or self-centred, but he was an essential anchor for every team he played for.

Off the field, Makélélé has continued to give back to the football community in impressive ways. He has worked as a coach for several teams, including Paris Saint-Germain and Eupen. He has also been involved in charity work, supporting organisations that help underprivileged children in Africa. Claude Makélélé has left a legacy as one of the best defensive midfielders in football history. He was a player who always put the team first and worked tirelessly to make sure it was successful. His style of play inspired a generation of football players and he even has a position named after him! His impact on the sport will never be forgotten.

Career Highlights: Two-time Spanish La Liga Championship Winner, One-time Champions League Winner, One-time Supercopa de España Winner, One-time UEFA Super Cup Winner, One-time Intercontinental Cup Winner, Two-time Premier League Championship Winner, One-time FA Cup Winner.

LUKA MODRIĆ

Full Name: Luka Modrić

Nickname: Cruyff of the Balkan

Born: September 9, 1985

Hometown: Zadar, Croatia

Height: 5'8" (173cm)

Position: Midfielder

Club Team: Real Madrid

Former Club Teams: Dinamo Zagreb, Tottenham Hotspur

Notable Quote: "I am lucky to have played with so many great players in my career, but the most important thing is always the team. We win and lose together."

Luka Modrić easily makes it onto this list. Luka goes about his business effortlessly on the pitch and makes the game look easy with his passing range that stands up against anyone who has ever played. Modrić has enjoyed a long, successful career, and at 37, is still playing at the top level.

Luka was born in Zadar, Croatia in 1985. Like all the others in the GOAT category, he had a passion for football from a young age. He would spend hours on the training field kicking a ball around and it was these countless hours of work that led him to become one of the world's greatest. He was noticed by coaches and scouts alike, and it wasn't long before a professional team came calling.

Modrić remained with his home town's youth team NK Zadar until 2002 when Dinamo Zagreb of Croatia offered him a contract. Luka was only 16 at the time so he didn't make his debut for Zagreb until 2005, after a couple of spells on loan at Zrinjski

Mostar and Inter Zapresic. He returned to Zagreb and almost immediately helped them to win three league titles in a row. He was also named 'Prva HNL Player of the Year' in 2007, meaning the best player in the top flight of Croatian football.

By 2008, Luka had his sights set on the Premier League. It was Tottenham Hotspur that stumped up the cash, with a club record transfer fee of 16 million pounds. Today, that would be a bargain for such a talented player, but in 2008, that was the highest fee Tottenham had ever paid for a player. As it turned out, it was the right move, although it took Luka a while to get going after suffering a knee injury not long into his time there. Soon enough, though, Modrić became a fan favourite, occupying the central midfield role in the number 14 shirt, the number worn by his footballing hero Johan Cruyff. He would occasionally play on the left but it was in central midfield where he was most effective. The following season of 2009/2010, Spurs went on to qualify for the UEFA Champions League for the first time in the club's history and made it to the quarter finals. It was a very successful time for the club. Manager Harry Redknapp said of Modrić, " [He's] a hell of a player and a manager's dream... He trains like a demon and never complains, will work with and without the ball on the field and can beat a defender with a trick or with a pass. He could get into any team in the top four."

Modrić remained loyal to the team that brought him to the Premier League, and although offers were coming in from bigger clubs, he said, "Tottenham Hotspur gave me my chance in the Premier League and I want to go on to achieve great success here with them. ... I have no interest in going anywhere. Last season's top-four finish was an indication of where we are as a club and I feel I can continue to improve and ... achieve everything I want to at Spurs."

However, by mid 2011, the offers had ramped up from London rivals Chelsea. By this point, Modrić was also keen for the move, but a bid of around 43 million pounds was turned down by Tottenham Chairman Daniel Levy. The 2012/13 season began without a deal. Luka wanted a move to Chelsea but on the final day of the transfer window, another 40 million pound bid was rejected.

It was Spanish giants Real Madrid that persuaded Tottenham to part with their star man for a fee of just 30 million, more than 10 million pounds less than the bid turned down from Chelsea. Real Madrid was led by charismatic tactician manager Jose Mourhino, and was considered one of the best starting XI's (eleven primary players) ever to grace the pitch, with team captain Iker Casillas in goal and a star-studded line-up, with the likes of Rafael Varane and Sergio Ramos at centre-back, Casemiro, Xavi Alonso and Mesut Ozil in midfield and Cristiano Ronaldo on the left wing, and finally, French beast Karim Benzema in the striker or centre forward role. It was hard to see where a new player would fit in, but Modrić wanted first team football. Unfortunately, after joining late in the transfer window and missing pre-season training with his new teammates, he found himself on the bench for the beginning of his career with the club.

After making a few appearances off the bench, Modrić was finally brought off the bench for good in March, in a Champions League round of 16 games against Manchester United. His team were a goal down when he came on in the second half and scored an equalising goal to put his team level. It was a beauty of a strike from 25 yards out and gave Real Madrid the momentum to win the game 2-1, knocking out Manchester United and advancing to the quarter finals. That night was a turning point in Modrić's career at Real Madrid, and he started in both semi-final matches against German side Borussia Dortmund. In the semi-final first leg, though, Luka was played as an attacking midfielder and did not have the impact he'd had in the previous game. His side lost 4-1, though they followed up with a 2-0 win in the reverse fixture (last match against Borussia Dortmund), where Modrić was a deeper midfielder who passed the ball and created chances for the attackers. He was much more suited in this role, although the 2-0 victory wasn't enough to overcome the 4-1 defeat.

Luka became a regular starter in midfield alongside Xavi Alonso. They made a formidable pair, often running rings around the competition. He also led his national team of Croatia to the World Cup Final against France in 2018. In December of that year, Modrić was awarded the Ballon d'Or award, given to the best player of the year, and it was the first time in the previous 10 years that it wasn't won by either Lionel Messi or Luka's Real Madrid teammate Cristiano Ronaldo!

Career Highlights: Five-time Champions League Winner, Five-time FIFA Club World Cup Winner, Four-time European Super Cup Winner, Three-time Spanish La Liga Championsip Winner, One-time Ballon d'Or Winner, Four-time UEFA Super Cup Winner, Two-time Copa del Rey Winner, Four-time Spanish Super Cup Winner, Seven-time Croatian Footballer of the Year, One-time UEFA Best Player in Europe.

CARLI ANNE LLOYD

Full Name: Carli Anne Lloyd

Born: July 16, 1982

Hometown: Delran Township, New Jersey, USA

Height: 5'7" (170cm)

Position: Midfielder

Club Team (retired): NJ/NY Gotham FC

Former Club Teams: Chicago Red Stars, Sky Blue FC, Houston Dash

Notable Quote: "My mindset's always been to be the hardest-working player, to give everything you have, no matter what."

Carli Lloyd is one of the most successful and decorated women's football players in history. She was born in 1982, in Delran Township, New Jersey, USA, and at five years old was already showing an interest in football—or soccer, as Americans call it. Her mother has said of her passion for football, "She always loved it and showed a lot of ability from an early age, but she also has always worked hard." Lloyd spent her childhood playing football but it was the 1999 FIFA Women's World Cup that would inspire her to become an international sporting sensation. Watching the USA team raise the trophy fueled Carli's dream that one day she would lift the trophy herself. She was a dedicated athlete throughout high school, known for her outstanding ability on the ball and impressive passing range. On top of her midfield duties, she was also a prolific goalscorer, scoring 26 goals and eight assists in 21 games in her senior year, and winning a record 18 of them.

Lloyd started at Rutgers University from 2001 to 2004, where she played for the Scarlett Knights in the first team. In her first season, she played every game and scored 15 goals, winning awards and accolades and even breaking records. She ended as the school's all time leader in points, with 117, and scored a total of 50 goals! It was inevitable, then, that she would go on to achieve great things, and in 2009 she began her professional career with the Chicago Red Stars.

While still in college, Carli represented her country in the USA national team, and between 2002 and 2005, won the Nordic Cup four times in a row. In the 2004 tournament, Carli scored twice and started every game, establishing her as a starter for the following year, during which she scored three goals. In 2005 she joined the senior team and on June 10 was called up for her debut against Ukraine. That was one of the proudest moments of her life, as she was unsure if she would even start. She had 20 minutes of playing time and the team won the game 7-nil! Seeing her name on the back of her shirt was an amazing feeling for Lloyd, and spurred her on to have a long career with the national team. Reflecting on this achievement a decade later, Carli said, "It was so cool and such an honor to see my name on the back of my jersey, knowing that the US crest was on the front. Here I am now, 200 caps later," she said with pride. "I still get that same feeling every time I put on my jersey. It is never a guarantee to be on this field having an opportunity to represent my country. I will never take it for granted." Lloyd went on to achieve great things with them, including being the top goalscorer in the Algarve Cup, with four goals. It wasn't the goalscoring that she was known for, though. As a midfielder, her ability to control the ball in the middle of the pitch and distribute it to her teammates was why she remained a key starter for the USA.

When Lloyd first watched the national team win the 1999 FIFA Women's World Cup, it would have been hard to believe that only eight years later she would play in the tournament herself! She got her chance in the 2007 FIFA Women's World Cup. The USA had not lost a game and were favourites to win. But the first game of the tournament ended that winning run as they tied the game 2-2 with North Korea. In the next match, however, they beat Sweden in an impressive 2-0 victory. They finished off the group stages with a 1-0 win over Nigeria, which sent them through to a nerve-wracking tie with England, who had just beaten Argentina 6-1 in the group stages. The first half finished nil-nil and fans around the world were probably expecting the game to go to extra time or even penalties, but in just 12 minutes, the USA scored three goals! England couldn't respond, and the USA team went through to the semi-finals with Brazil.

They lost to Brazil 4-0, sending them into the third place play-off, which they won against Norway, 4-1. Third place will never be enough for a top athlete, though, and for Carli, it was all the motivation she needed to work harder to achieve her goals.

In the following 2011 World Cup, the national team had their revenge on Brazil by knocking them out in the quarter finals, winning 5-3 on penalties. Unfortunately, they lost on penalties themselves in the final to Japan. Time and time again, though, these painful events in Lloyd's career only seemed to make her stronger. In the 2015 World Cup, she was named captain for four of the fixtures, including in her 200th cap (appearance) for the national team, and she scored the winning goal in the quarter finals against China. The semi-finals will be remembered for Lloyd's freedom of attack and ability to control the ball in midfield, something she has done throughout her career. They beat Germany 2-0, which put them into the final against none other than the team that had knocked them out at the final hurdle last time around - Japan. The Japanese had beaten England in the semi-finals and were ready to win the World Cup for the second consecutive time. But then Carli Lloyd did something that hadn't been done in either the men's or the women's game since Geoff Hurst did it in 1966.

If you're a fan of English football, you probably know that 1966 was the last time the England men's team won the FIFA World Cup. In that game, Geoff Hurst scored three goals, or a 'hat-trick', as it is known. Since then, no other professional player had scored a hat-trick in a World Cup final. And while Hurst scored two of his goals in extra time, when the game was tied after 90 minutes, Lloyd managed to score three goals in just 13 minutes! Nobody remembers much else about that match that ended 5-2, which included an own goal (a goal scored inadvertently by the defense) from the USA. This incredible achievement further cemented Carli Lloyd as one of the best players to ever play the game.

Though Lloyd had a successful professional club career with the Chicago Red Stars and quickly became one of the team's star players, she is best known for her time with the US Women's National Team. She has also been a key player in the Olympics, helping lead the US to gold medal victories in the 2008, 2012, and 2021 Olympics. She scored two goals in the gold medal match of the 2012 Olympics, including a stunning 54-yard strike that has become one of the most iconic moments in women's football history. Throughout her career, Lloyd has been recognised for her talent and hard work. She has been named FIFA Women's Player of the Year twice and US Football Female Athlete of the Year six times.

Lloyd has been a vocal advocate for women's football and gender equality in sports. She has spoken out about the need for equal pay and better working conditions for female athletes, and encourages girls to pursue their dreams on and off the field. She is known for her tenacity, her work ethic, and her ability to inspire and motivate her teammates. For Lloyd, football is not just a job or a sport, but a passion and a way of life.

Career Highlights: Two-time Olympic Gold Medalist, Two-time FIFA Women's World Cup Champion, Two-time FIFA Player of the Year, Four-time Olympian, One-time US Soccer Athlete of the Year, Four-time SheBelieves Cup Winner.

JOHAN CRUYFF

Full Name: Hendrik Johannes Cruijff

Nickname: Johan

Born: April 25, 1947

Died: March 24, 2016

Hometown: Amsterdam, Netherlands

Height: 5'11" (180 cm)

Position: Forward/Midfielder

Club Team (at time of retirement): Feyenoord Rotterdam

Former Club Teams: Ajax Amsterdam, FC Barcelona, Los Angeles Aztecs, Washington Diplomats, Levante UD, Feyenoord Rotterdam

Johan Cruyff, born Hendrik Johannes Cruijff on April 25, 1947, was a Dutch footballer and coach widely regarded by many as one of the greatest players in the history of the sport. He was also regarded as one of the best managers of all time. He was born in Amsterdam, Netherlands and grew up in a working-class family. As with all GOATs, Cruyff's love for football began at an early age. As a child, he spent countless hours playing the game with his friends. Football, however, wasn't Cruyff's favourite sport. He actually preferred baseball and played it until he was 15 years old, when his football coaches, who saw something special in him, told him that he had to make a choice. He joined the local football club, Ajax Amsterdam. In fact, he lived five minutes from the stadium of one of the biggest teams in the Netherlands! On Johan's 10th birthday, he joined the Ajax youth team and quickly rose through the ranks.

At the age of 12, Cruyff sadly lost his father and decided to use football to pay tribute to him. He wanted to make his dad proud and as a result, became a legend.

Cruyff made his professional debut for Ajax in 1964, at just 17. His team lost 3-1 but Johan stood out among his teammates and scored Ajax's only goal of the game against GVAV. Unfortuanetely, Ajax had their worst season in the history of the entire club, finishing 13th in the Eredivisie Dutch League, which was very disappointing. But Cruyff quickly established himself as a key player, and the following season in 1965/66, he scored 25 goals in just 23 games. This was a much more satisfactory season for Johan, who helped his team bounce back from the worst year in their history to winning the league. The following year, Johan bagged 33 goals, making him the league's top goalscorer and winning him the golden boot. They also won the KNVB Cup, the first time Johan had won the double, something he would go on to do again three years later.

Cruyff was known for his exceptional technical skills, including his dribbling, passing, and vision on the pitch. I remember learning the 'Cruyff turn' as a child in school, a move that involved feinting one way before quickly turning in the opposite direction to evade defenders. We used to practise it in training and at break times and wondered who this player was who was good enough to invent skill moves that remained a part of the game years later. Johan was also one of the main players respon-sible for creating a style of play called 'Total Football,' developed by Ajax in the 1970's by former Ajax player and manager Rinus Michels and followed as a philosophy by Cruyff throughout his playing career as well as his managing career.

Total Football was a style of play that allowed any player on the pitch to take on the role of another player, so rather than each player sticking to a fixed position, it allowed more freedom to roam and pick up the ball and run into other areas. This style suited Cruyff to a tee, as he was able to pick up the ball in midfield and dribble into the danger zone of his opponents, knowing that the players around him could cover him if he lost the ball. This gave him the confidence to express himself on the pitch like no other player had before. But Cruyff was a team player and also used the philosophy of Total Football to get back and defend when his team was being counter-attacked.

Cruyff wore the number 9 shirt regularly, and it was rare for any player to wear anything other than numbers 1-11, so when he was injured in the 1970/71 season, the number 9 was worn by team-mate Gerrie Muhren. When Cruyff returned in October of that year, he wore the number 14. He scored in that game and his team won 1-0, so he kept the number 14 from then on. That season, Ajax won the European Cup, which is now the Champions League. The team dominated Europe in the early '70s, mainly because the Total Football strategy was so effective when mastered by players like Cruyff. They went on to win the Champions League Cup three years running, in 1971, '72, defeating Inter Milan in the final, and '73, with a victory over Juventus. Cruyff was named Ballon d'Or winner in '71, '73 and '74. It was an amazing time in football, and it was dominated by the Dutch.

In 1973, Johan played his last match for Ajax in a 6-1 defeat to FC Amsterdam. He then went to FC Barcelona, who paid 6 million guilders, which was less than 2 million pounds, but in those days was a world record-breaking transfer. He instantly became a favourite with the fans, whose devotion to him increased when he named his son Jordi, a name that comes from the Catalan region of Spain. (His son would also become a great player, making appearances for Barcelona and Manchester United.) While playing for Barcelona, Johan helped them win the league title for the first time in 14 years. He also scored a goal that was dubbed *Le but impossible de Cruyff* (Cruyff's impossible goal), which was an amazing show of athletic ability from Johan, who leapt into the air, virtually at head height, and kicked the ball into the net with the back of his heel, sending the ball past Atlético Madrid goalie Miguel Reina.

In 1978, Cruyff retired from football. However, after his retirement, he was persuaded to invest a large sum of money in pig farms! Yes, pig farms. Unfortunately, the investment turned out to be a scam and Johan lost millions of pounds, which forced him to return to football to recoup some of his losses.

Cruyff moved to the United States, where he played for the Los Angeles Aztecs and the Washington Diplomats in the North American Soccer League. He also had a brief stint with Levante UD in Spain before returning to the Netherlands to play for his boyhood club, Ajax Amsterdam, and later Feyenoord Rotterdam, where he retired for good in 1984.

Upon retirement as a player, Johan became manager of Ajax, just as his former manager Rinus Michels had done before him. He coached a fresh young Ajax team to victory in a European Cup, where they won 1-0 against Locomotive Leipzig from East Germany. Cruyff joined Barcelona as coach in 1988/89, where he developed his style of play from a manager's perspective and really put his stamp on the game. He implemented his style of play to the first team but also the reserve teams, which made it easier for youth players to integrate into the team. In addition to developing youth talent, Cruyff brought in players such as Pep Guardiola, Ron Koeman, Michael Laudrup, Hristo Stoichkov, Georghe Hagi and Brazilian superstar Romario. Ajax won many trophies under Cruyff, including one European Cup, four Liga championships, one Cup Winners' Cup, one Copa del Rey and four Supercopa de España.

Between 1991 and 1994, Barcelona won four league titles in a row and also won the European Cup. They were classed as one of the greatest football teams in history and Johan's philosophy of Total Football drove everything they did. Even in today's game, you can see how much of an impact Cruyff has had, including for bringing Pep Guardiola into the team and developing him into a captain and then a manager. Pep took the philosophy even further with Barcelona and then brought it to England when he joined Manchester City. The style is incredibly effective, and as part of Cruyff's dream team, Pep knew exactly how to master it.

Career Highlights: One-time Intercontinental Cup Winner, Three-time European Champion Clubs' Cup Winner, Seven-time KNVB Cup Winner, One-time Spanish La Liga Champion, Three-time Champions League Cup Winner, Three-time Ballon d'Or Winner, One-time UEFA Super Cup Winner, One-time Spanish Cup Winner, Six-time Dutch Cup Winner, Nine-time Dutch Champion.

LIONEL ANDRÉS MESSI

Nickname: Messiah

Born: June 24, 1987

Hometown: Rosario, Argentina

Height: 5'7" (170cm)

Position: Forward

Club Team: Paris Saint-Germain

Former Club Teams: FC Barcelona

Notable Quote: "I have fun like a child in the street. When the day comes when I'm not enjoying it, I will leave football."

Lionel Messi is known around the world as one of the greatest ball dribblers of all time. He was born on June 24, 1987, in Rosario, Argentina. He joined his local club, Newell's Old Boys, when he was six years old! During his six years at the club, he racked up almost 500 goals and was part of a youth squad dubbed 'The Machine of 87', for the year the players in the team were born. They were an unstoppable force and Messi's natural talent was evident from early on. Lionel's father, a manager in a steel factory, coached his son from an early age but it was Messi's grandmother who took him to training sessions. She died just before he turned 11, and ever since, whenever he scores a goal, he looks up and points to the sky in tribute to her.

Messi had a medical condition called growth hormone disorder (GHD) that stopped him from growing properly. The treatment he needed was expensive but his family couldn't afford it. Luckily, his football skills caught the attention of scouts from FC Barcelona and they agreed to pay for the treatment. At 13, Messi was offered a spot in the youth academy at Barcelona, which meant moving to Spain from his home in Argentina. This was a chance for Lionel, also known as Leo, to join one of the best youth academies in the world. He later said, "It wasn't difficult for me to move to Barcelona because I knew I had to. I needed money for my medicine to help me grow and Barcelona was the only club that offered. So as soon as they did, I knew I had to go."

Messi was successful during his time with the youth team and was seen as a future star by the coaches and staff. He would have to work hard for another four years, though, before he was able to join the first team. In the 2003/04 season, Leo climbed through the ranks, playing one match for the Juvinilles B Team before being promoted to the Juvinilles A Team, where he played 11 games and scored 18 goals.

In 2004, at 16, Leo made his debut for FC Barcelona in a friendly match against FC Porto. Jose Mourinho was in charge of Porto at the time and Leo impressed him. After the friendly, he trained daily with the Barcelona B Team and weekly with the first team. One of the first team players was Brazilian legend Ronaldhino, who took a liking to Messi, and told him he thought Messi would become better than him one day. He called Leo 'little brother', which helped to ease Messi into the first team. During the 03/04 season, Messi played games for Barcelona C and B, Juvinilles B and A, and also the friendly for the first team. He scored a total of 36 goals across all teams, helped Juvinilles B to a league title and saved Barcelona C from relegation (being moved to a lower division).

In October 2004, Ronaldhino and the other first team players asked manager Frank Rijkaard to promote Messi to the first team, and he listened. Messi, who is left-footed, started as a substitute, playing in a right wing position. Although this wasn't his preferred position at first, he quickly learned how to cut inside and shoot with his stronger left foot. He came on in nine games that season and was the youngest ever player for Barcelona to play in a competitive match. He even came on as a sub in a UEFA Champions League game against Shakhtar Donetsk, where his 'older brother' Ronaldhino assisted him with his first goal. Scoring that goal against Albacete in a 2-0 win for Barcelona was a proud moment for Leo, who, when asked about his favourite goal of his career, said, "My favourite is my first in La Liga. At the time, I had something to prove and I wanted to say thanks to the coach and to Barcelona. But that might change if I score in the World Cup final one day." He went on to score three goals in the World Cup final in Qatar 2022, so would likely have a different answer to that question today! That was Messi's last performance in a FIFA World Cup but he helped his team to victory. It was a perfect way to cap off his international career.

Before the 2005/06 started, Messi took part in a pre-season tournament where his team faced a strong Juventus side managed by ex-England manager Fabio Capello. Capello was impressed with Messi's performance and wanted to take him on loan for the season; however, Inter Milan were also interested in Messi, who at the time had a 150 million pound release clause. If a club pays the release clause, and the player agrees, then the player can move without having to negotiate with Barcelona. Inter Milan saw the potential in Messi and agreed to pay the 150 million pounds. They began negotiations with Messi but he wasn't interested, even though they offered to pay triple his current wages! Leo was loyal to the club that had helped him receive the treatment he needed and that nurtured him as a player. Barcelona repaid him by updating his contract for the second time in three months, keeping him signed to the club until 2014.

He went on to achieve great things with Barcelona, although the team began to decline over the years. Messi suffered a few injuries during this period, and missed out on the UEFA Champions League final, which wasa huge disappointment for him. He continued to improve, though, and the Spanish media dubbed him 'Messiah'. His team, on the other hand, were not always performing at their best and a few poor seasons led to manager Rijkaard and Ronaldhino leaving the club.

Messi was given the number 10 shirt the following season by new manager and former Barcelona captain Pep Guardiola, and was also given a new training regime and diet to help him to reduce injuries. It seemed to work, as he was injury-free for most of the next few years. He just missed out on winning the Ballon d'Or and FIFA Player of the Year in 2008, coming runner-up in both to Cristiano Ronaldo. There has always been a friendly rivalry between the two, in part created by the media and those debating the world's best player, since both names are first on most people's lips when the question is asked: 'Messi or Ronaldo?'

During the 2008/09 season, the first season Messi was without injuries, he scored 38 goals in 51 appearances for the club. Between him, Thierry Henry and Samuel Eto'o, they racked up 100 goals that season! One of the best moments of that season was winning 6-2 at the Bernabeu Stadium, the home of their fiercest rivals, Real Madrid. When these two teams play, the game is known as 'El Clásico'. This victory is still Barcelona's biggest win at their rivals' home. That was not the peak of the season for Barcelona, though, who had struggled in recent years. With the help of Lionel Messi, they were on the way to becoming a world-beating team, just like the 'Machine of 87' from his youth. They won the Copa Del Rey, a Spanish club tournament, and then three days later were crowned league champions. They were still in the Champions League and winning that gave them 'the treble'. It was a feat that had not been achieved since Peter Schmeichel's Manchester United side in 1999, and was the first time in history the treble had been won by a Spanish team.

In May 2009, Barcelona beat Manchester United in the final of the Champions League, winning 2-0, with Lionel scoring the second goal, a header over Edwin Van Der Sarr, one of the world's best goalkeepers. For his performance, Messi earned a new contract with the club that would run until 2016 and had a new release clause of 250 million pounds. He went on to help Barcelona win a record six trophies in one year, which included the treble of the previous season, the Supercopa de España and UEFA Super Cup in August of 2009, topping it off in December of that year with the FIFA World Cup. Leo scored the winning goal in that game, hitting the ball off his chest and into the net of Estudiantes de La Plata.

Messi also became a key player for the Argentine national team. He made his debut for the team in 2005, at 18, and quickly became a fan favourite. He has since gone on to lead the team to numerous titles, including the Copa America in 2021, his first major international trophy with the team. They also won the FIFA World Cup in Qatar in 2022, in a game that will be remembered as one of the greatest World Cup finals ever played. In that game, which lasted 120 minutes after extra time, Messi stepped up to put his penalty in the back of the net. This was the third of his three goals, the first of which was also a penalty in normal time. Messi became the first player to score a goal in every round of the tournament since the round of 16 knockout stage was added in 1986.

The final was a rollercoaster for Leo; his team went a goal up from his penalty and then teammate Angel Di Maria put them two up, and everything looked like it was going their way when the halftime whistle blew. But anything can happen in football! France came out a different team in the second half and got back into the game with two goals from young superstar, French striker Kylian Mbappé. Argentina had no response, which sent the game into extra time. That is, until Messi popped up in the 108th minute with a goal that looked certain to send them back to Argentina as champions. It became a battle between Messi at one end and Mbappé at the other, and it wasn't long before young

Kylian equalised for France, putting the score at 3-3 and sending the match into penalties. It was down to Leo's teammates to win it. Luckily, they didn't let him down. The winning penalty was scored by Gonzalo Montiel, and Messi's lifelong dream was complete. He had achieved everything possible at club level, staying with Barcelona throughout his career until finally moving to Paris Saint-Germain (PSG) and playing alongside Kylian Mbappé, providing him with a mentor and a role model, just as Ronaldhino had done for him years earlier.

Messi remains a fan favourite around the world, and his impact on the game will be felt for generations to come.

Career Highlights: Seven-time Ballon d'Or Winner, Three-time UEFA Best Player in Europe, 10-time Player of the Year, Three-time Best FIFA Men's Player, Four-time Champions League Winner, One-time Copa America Winner, Three-time FIFA Club World Cup Winner, 10-time Spanish Champion, Three-time UEFA Super Cup Winner, Seven-time Spanish Cup Winner, One-time Olympic Medalist.

4

FOOTBALL'S GREATEST MOMENTS

Football is known for its unpredictability and has made much use out of the saying 'anything can happen.' In this section, we are going to look at some of the times when something *did* happen. This is a collection of some of the greatest goals and footballing moments that the game has to offer.

DIEGO MARADONA'S "HAND OF GOD" GOAL (1986)

Although I was less than a year old at the time, this moment was one that stuck with me for my entire life. I can't remember seeing it on TV at the time but looking back over the years, it has been a goal shown in some form at every World Cup since. It was way back in 1986, during the World Cup quarter-final match between Argentina and England, when Argentinian superstar Diego Maradona scored one of the most controversial goals in football history. The incident occurred in the 51st minute of the match, when Maradona used his left hand to punch the ball into the net, beating England's goalkeeper Peter Shilton.

At the time, Maradona claimed the goal was scored with his head, but in a post-match interview, he famously referred to it as the

"Hand of God". While the goal was technically illegal, the referee did not see the handball and the goal stood. This is where VAR would have stepped in and disallowed the goal in today's game, but in 1986, the England team didn't have that luxury and instead had to concede a goal that many of the players at the time actually saw bouncing off Maradona's hand. Despite the controversy, Maradona's "Hand of God" goal remains one of the most iconic moments in football history. It was a display of Maradona's quick thinking and determination to win, as he managed to outsmart the England defence and score a crucial goal for his team.

For young football fans, the "Hand of God" goal serves as a lesson about the importance of fair play and sportsmanship. While Maradona's goal may have been a clever move, it was ultimately against the rules of the game. It's important for young players to understand that cheating and dishonesty have no place in football or any other sport.

Maradona could have easily gone into my list of greatest of all time, as he was such a skilful player. I remember hearing England striker Gary Lineker talking about training with Diego. He spoke of how he could do 'kick ups' with the ball for hours, and whenever he felt like it, he would blast the ball about 100 feet in the air and casually wait for it to land, where he would catch it on the volley without letting it touch the ground, and then carry on with his kick ups. Even superstars of the game were amazed at the abilities of Maradona and the way he could control a ball.

Overall, the "Hand of God" goal will go down in history as one of the most memorable and controversial moments in football. It continues to be discussed and debated by fans and experts to this day, and is a reminder of why VAR is so important, even if it goes against us.

LIONEL MESSI'S GOAL VS GETAFE (2007)

In 2007, Messi scored what many consider to be one of the greatest goals in football history during a Copa Del Rey match against Getafe.

I remember watching Messi picking up the ball near the halfway line and dribbling past four Getafe players before slotting the ball past the goalkeeper. The way he weaved through the Getafe defence with such ease and grace was quite literally incredible. Messi's goal was not just a display of his individual talent, but also of his incredible speed, agility, and creativity. It showcased what makes football such an exciting and captivating sport, as one player was able to take on an entire team and come out victorious.

For young football fans, Messi's goal serves as a source of inspiration and motivation. It shows that with hard work, dedication, and a little bit of creativity, anything is possible on the football pitch.

Overall, Messi's goal versus Getafe is a moment that will be remembered for years to come as a testament to his incredible skill and talent as a football player. It continues to inspire young players and fans alike to pursue their dreams and never give up on their goals.

RYAN GIGGS' GOAL VS ARSENAL (1999)

In the 1999 FA Cup semi-final replay between Manchester United and Arsenal, Ryan Giggs scored one of the most iconic goals in football history. With the score tied at 1-1 in extra time, Giggs picked up the ball near the halfway line, dribbled past several Arsenal defenders, and then blasted the ball past the Arsenal goalkeeper to give Manchester United a 2-1 win.

Giggs' goal was not only a stunning display of individual skill, but it also helped propel Manchester United to one of their most successful seasons ever. The team went on to win the FA Cup, Premier League, and Champions League titles that year, cementing their place in football history. For young football fans, Giggs' goal is a symbol of the power of hard work. Despite facing a tough Arsenal defence, Giggs never gave up and continued to push forward until he was able to score the match-winning goal.

What this goal meant to the millions of Manchester United fans around the world can't be put into words. The rivalry between the two clubs was one of the fiercest in modern footballing times, as they were regarded as the two top teams of the period. Manchester United were on the verge of winning the treble and Arsenal were approaching their peak, which would come a few years later, when they won the 2003/04 season with 26 of their 38 league matches and drew the remaining 12, meaning they didn't lose a single game for an entire season! Add that to the undefeated run they'd started at the end of the previous season and it was 49 games without defeat for Arsenal and manager Arsène Wenger. Ironically, that run was halted by none other than Manchester United, who were desperate to claim top spot again after Arsenal had dominated the last season.

There was also the rivalry between defensive midfielders Roy Keane of Manchester United and Patrick Viera of Arsenal. The two players appeared to hate each other on the pitch and it was always entertaining to watch them go head to head. Both were tough and took no prisoners, and this only heated up the rivalry between the two clubs, which made Ryan Giggs' wonder goal even sweeter.

Brazil's 1970 World Cup team goal is widely regarded as one of the most iconic and beautiful goals in football history. It was scored in the final of the 1970 World Cup tournament. Brazil was facing Italy in the final, and they went on to win the match 4-1, with this particular goal being a standout moment of the match.

The goal was scored by Carlos Alberto Torres, who was the captain of the Brazilian team. It began with a corner kick taken by Rivelino, which was swung into the edge of the Italian penalty box. The ball was then chested down by the Brazilian midfielder Clodoaldo, who was under pressure from four Italian players.

What followed was a master class in teamwork and individual skill. Clodoaldo dribbled past all four Italian players, weaving his way through their defences with ease. He then passed the ball to Jairzinho, who had sprinted up the right wing. He was known for his pace and ability to outrun players even when he had the ball. Jairzinho quickly crossed the ball towards the centre of the penalty area, where Pele, Brazil's star player, had made a perfectly timed run.

Pele leapt into the air and headed the ball towards the Italian goal, but his effort was blocked by the Italian goalkeeper, Enrico Albertosi. However, the ball fell straight for Carlos Alberto, who had been charging forward from his position as right back. Alberto struck the ball with his right foot, sending it into the back of the net with power and precision.

The Brazilian players celebrated wildly, hugging each other and jumping up and down in excitement. The goal was a moment of pure magic, showcasing the incredible skill, teamwork, and creativity of Brazil's 1970 World Cup team. It wasn't just the brilliance of one player, as we have seen for most of these goals, but a case where the team all pulled together with one aim and scored the goal. Now and then, these teams seem to come together, such as the European machine of Ajax in the 70's; the Manchester United team that went on to win the treble, who mostly came from the same academy and were dubbed 'the class of '92'; and even my own team Nottingham Forest, who, despite having very little money in comparison to other European clubs in the late 70's and early 80's, managed to win back to back European Cups under manager Brian Clough. This Brazilian team was another example of one of these teams.

What made this goal so special was the way it was scored. It was a perfect example of teamwork, with each player contributing to the goal in their own unique way. Clodoaldo's dribbling skills were incredible, as he managed to weave his way through four Italian defenders with ease. Jairzinho's cross was perfectly timed and placed, allowing Pele to make a run into the box. Pele's header was saved, but Carlos Alberto was in the right place at the right time to score the goal.

Every player involved was a superstar in their own right, with incredible skill, speed, and technical ability. Pele was widely regarded as the greatest footballer of all time, while Jairzinho was one of the fastest players in the tournament. Clodoaldo was a gifted midfielder with incredible dribbling skills, and Carlos Alberto was a talented defender who could also attack with great effect.

The goal was a testament to the quality of the Brazilian team as a whole, and their ability to work together as a unit. They played with a sense of style, flair, and creativity that was unmatched by any other team in the tournament. They were not just a team of individual stars, but a team that played with a sense of unity and purpose.

Brazil's 1970 World Cup team goal captured the essence of football, with its blend of individual brilliance and teamwork, and it remains an iconic moment in the history of the sport.

ZINEDINE ZIDANE'S GOAL IN THE 2002 CHAMPIONS LEAGUE FINAL

The 2002 Champions League Final between Real Madrid and Bayer Leverkusen was a tense and closely fought match, with both teams fighting hard to gain the upper hand. But in the 45th minute of the game, Zinedine Zidane of Real Madrid scored one of the most incredible goals in football history on a cross from Roberto Carlos, another legend of the game from Brazil who played as right back for Real Madrid. He had an amazing ability to put the ball anywhere he desired and once scored one of the craziest goals in football himself, which we will discuss later. In this game, though, the ball came from Carlos and toward Zidane, who was standing just outside the penalty box. With one swift movement, Zidane unleashed a stunning volley with his left foot that rocketed into the back of the net, leaving the goalkeeper with no chance. Zidane ran to the touchline in a display of pure emotion; he couldn't believe he had just scored what would go down as one of the greatest goals in the tournament's history. The powerful volley from the edge of the 18-yard box was such a stunning goal that it even surprised him!

Zidane's goal was not only a display of his incredible technique and skill, but showcased his ability to perform under pressure. The Champions League is the biggest club competition in European football and scoring in the final is every boy's dream. I'm sure that as a child Zinedine had visualised a similar moment in his dreams, but I wonder if he actually believed it would come true. Let that be a lesson to anyone reading this with a dream of achieving great things in football or anything else you choose to do. If you train and practise hard enough, it can be done. Zinedine wanted to achieve his dreams and in that moment, he knew he had accomplished something special. The goal helped give Real Madrid a 2-1 victory and secured their place as champions of Europe.

MANCHESTER UNITED'S TREBLE WIN 1999

Sometimes, it's not what you do, but how you do it. In the case of Manchester United and their 'class of '92' side who grew up and developed together in the Manchester United youth academy, it's both what they did and how they did it, as they managed a spectacular achievement in the most outstanding fashion. First of all, let's take a minute to refresh our understanding and appreciation for what it takes to win 'the treble.' First of all, you need to win a domestic cup tournament, which means you must win a set of knockout games until you reach the final, and if you lose at any stage, you're out. Then you must win your domestic league. This is achieved over the course of the entire season; in United's case that was 38 games in the Premiere League, arguably the toughest league in the world, and to be crowned league champions, you must have more points than any other team. This must also be done in the top league of your country, as only the top teams of the top leagues are allowed entry into the Champions League, which if you're a European club is the highest achievement in football. If you qualified for the Champions League, you would have had to have finished at the top or near the top of your league in the previous season.

United had won the FA Cup and they had just been named league champions; now the icing on the cake was to win the Champions League, having already made it to the final.

It was May 26th, 1999 and the stage was set at Camp Nou in Barcelona, one of the largest stadiums in the world. German giants Bayern Munich were the team that stood in the way of history being made for Manchester United, and after beating fellow Germans FC Kaiserslautern in the quarter-finals and Dynamo Kiev of Ukraine in the semi-finals, they weren't going to be easy to break down. This was also the third time in the competition that the two teams had met, having shared the points on both meetings in the group stages, with the first game in Germany ending 2-2 and the reverse fixture at Old Trafford finishing a 1-1 draw. Bayern Munich were also league champions in the Bundesliga, after only losing four games all season. There was not a lot between these two powerhouses of European football.

When the first whistle blew, all the tension and pre-game nerves went out the window and the Manchester United players had 90 minutes to secure a place in history. It was Bayern Munich, though, that looked the better team in the opening stages and after just six minutes, forward Basler put his team ahead with a free kick that caught goalkeeper Peter Schmiechel off guard. United were a goal down and although they kept hold of the ball well, they failed to produce anything at the other end of the pitch. In the second half, a few more chances were lost for both teams, with goalkeepers keeping the score at 1-0 which, with the clock ticking, wasn't good enough for Manchester United manager Sir Alex Ferguson. Changes had to be made to cope with the attacks of Basler and his teammates and after bringing on Teddy Sherringham earlier in the second half, with just ten minutes to go, Ferguson brought on Norwiegan striker Ole Gunnar Solksjaer.

Ole was a young and enthusiastic player with loads of skill and had been called on from the bench in the past to get United out of sticky situations. This was, without a doubt, the toughest challenge they'd had to face as a team and the next 10 minutes would go on to become one of the most memorable periods in world football. Solkjaer immediately made an impact and forced the keeper Kahn to make a great save. Seconds later, Munich went up the other end of the pitch and almost secured the victory as German international striker Janker made a spectacular overhead kick that bounced off the crossbar. United had a couple more chances to draw level in the last five minutes, which would have sent the game into extra time and possible penalties but the 90 minutes was up and the game was in injury time.

Injury time is where all of the stoppages in the normal 90 minutes are added up and added on to the end of normal time. Throughout this particular 90 minutes, three minutes of injury time was given by the referee, meaning they had three minutes to score. Otherwise, Bayern Munich would be crowned champions of Europe. If United managed to score in three minutes, the game would be a draw and would be forced into extra time, which is two more periods of 15 minutes of play and a five minute break in between.

Half a minute into injury time, United won a corner kick, and football superstar David Beckham swung the ball into the box destined for the head of an attacker. Even Peter Schmiechel had made it from his goal area to join the attackers in the box, willing to throw everything on the line to get the goal they needed. The ball missed the head of any of his teammates but Bayern Munich failed to clear the ball far enough and it fell to the feet of Ryan Giggs, who made an effort to shoot but it was a weak attempt that turned out to be a pass to his teammate Teddy Sheringham, who struck the ball and flew it into the back of the net in the bottom corner. The roof lifted off the stadium as Manchester United had forced the game into extra time against all odds and with Bayern Munich looking like the better team for the majority of the game. The Germans couldn't believe what had happened and were shocked at the fact that they would have to play another 30 minutes of football and score another goal if they were going to lift the trophy that they had all but won just moments earlier.

There was also two and a half minutes of normal time yet to be played and a bewildered Bayern Munich let Manchester United get up the pitch once again and force another corner. This time, the goal keeper stayed put as they were happy to take the game to extra time and didn't want to leave themselves open to a counter attack that could quickly undo everything they had worked for. With about 45 seconds left on the clock, David Beckham took the corner again, this time finding the head of goalscorer Teddy Sheringham. Teddy headed the ball across the face of the goal, more in the hope of finding a player to knock the ball into the net rather than going for goal himself, and managed to find super-sub Ole Gunnar Solkjaer, who got a touch on the ball and sent it into the roof of the net! Three minutes ago they were looking at defeat, and now they were on the verge of winning not only this massive game but the treble as well.

The Bayern Munich players, captained by Lothar Matthäus, were left devastated and could barely pick themselves up off the ground to continue the last few seconds of the match. When the final whistle was blown, the roar of the crowd was ear-splitting, as the result had already been decided in everyone's head. The tournament organisers had even secured the red and blue ribbons of Bayern Munich onto the trophy in preparation. Fans who had been jumping for joy were now in despair and those who had lost hope were now screaming at the top of their lungs in victory. The scene at the Nou Camp that night will be difficult to replicate again and the achievements of Ole and his team in the face of adversity are a lesson for anyone facing a tough challenge.

MANCHESTER CITY VS QPR 2011/12 FINAL DAY

The final day of the season is always filled with drama at both ends of the table (the chart that ranks teams based on points scored), no matter what level you are playing. With relegation fears looming for those at the bottom of the table and dreams of becoming league champions at the top, the last match can sometimes be the deciding factor between success and failure. In this match in the 2011/12 season between Manchester City and Queens Park Rangers, decisions were made at both ends. QPR were one place above the relegation zone in 17th with 20th, 19th and 18th all being relegated to the Championship, which is the second tier in English football. Two points separated them from Bolton Wanderers in 17th, and having much better goal difference than Wanderers, a draw against City would be all they needed to secure survival in the Premier League.

That would be easier said than done, though, as Manchester City were top of the Premier League and on track to win the league for the first time since its creation in 1991. Chasing City for the title were local rivals Manchester United, who had the same number of points as City and were only behind on goal difference, having scored two less and conceded six more than City going into the final game. If City could equal Manchester United's points, it should have been enough to claim the league title. However, football's a funny old game and never quite goes how you expect it. The rivalry between the two Manchester clubs was intense. Leading up to the game, United boss Alex Ferguson described City as 'the noisy neighbours,' stating that in his lifetime they would never become the great team that Manchester United was. This added fuel to the fire and gave the blue half of Manchester even more determination to keep hold of their lead in the league and go on to win the title.

The game got underway at City's stadium, The Ethihad, in front of the live TV cameras and 48,000 fans, most of them home supporters hoping to see their team make history. Everything was going according to plan for City as defender Zabaletta opened the scoring with his first goal of the season. I'm sure if he could have picked one game to score in all season, this would have most certainly been it. The stakes were high and he had just given a blow to QPR, who had further bad news when Bolton Wanderers went ahead in their game. As things stood, they were currently in the bottom three and on their way down. Manchester City, on the other hand, were top of the table and on their way to becoming Premier League Champions for the first time. By halftime, rivals Manchester United were leading in their match against Sunderland and City needed to keep their lead if they were to achieve their dreams. By contrast, QPR had to give it everything they had if they wanted to stay in the league and avoid relegation. They didn't have to wait long before being given an opportunity, as Joleon Lescott tried to clear the ball with his head and didn't get it quite right. The ball fell for Djiril Cisse, a talented attacker who didn't need a second chance against City keeper and England international Joe Hart, slotting it past him the first time to give his team a glimmer of hope. That goal put them back outside of the relegation zone and if they could hold on, they would be safe.

Tensions were high and emotions were getting the better of some players when Joey Barton received a straight red card without warning for elbowing City ace Carlos Tevez in the face. The ref on the day, Mike Dean, didn't hesitate to issue the red to Barton, who may have just thrown everything away for his team in a moment of madness. Sometimes emotions can get the better of you in sport and this is a lesson in what not to do. Barton acted surprised when the ref pulled out the red and when he eventually left the pitch, the sinking feeling of regret would have been with him for the rest of the match as he watched it on TV from the dressing room. Rangers were now down to ten men against a City team that were top of the league and easily capable of scoring against any eleven players, never mind ten. Despite all the odds, the rest of the Queens Park Rangers team had a job to do. They needed to soak up the pressure that Manchester City were putting on them and look for any opportunity to form some kind of attack. In the 66th minute of the game, Rangers forward Jamie Mackie got his head on the end of a cross from Armand Traore, which he managed to direct past Joe Hart and into the back of the net, putting QPR 2-1 ahead. With 24 minutes of normal time remaining, they needed to hold on to the lead, or at least not lose the game, and survival would be theirs.

With Manchester United ahead against Sunderland and City now losing, it was looking like United's day to snatch the title from under City's noses. As news of the other fixtures made its way across the other grounds involved, fans knew they were in for an afternoon full of ups and downs, and the best was yet to come. City piled on the pressure, giving keeper Paddy Kenny the chance to put in one of the finest performances of his career. Save after save, he kept his team in the lead after a relentless attack from City. In the game between Bolton Wanderers and Stoke City at the other end of the table, Stoke had just equalised the game at 2-2, and if that stayed the same, QPR would be safe even if they lost to City. The players didn't want to leave anything to chance, though, and kept the league leaders at bay for the remainder of the 90 minutes. The referee called five additional minutes of injury time and this was City's last chance to get something out of this game that was looking more and more out of reach as the seconds ticked on. They managed to win a corner with just three of the five minutes to go and striker Djzeko headed the ball into the back of the net past Kenny to make the game a 2-2 draw. They quickly picked the ball out from the back of the net and ran up the pitch to restart the game.

Rangers took the kick-off from the restart and just booted the ball up the pitch into Manchester City's half and out for a throw-in. Joe Hart ran from his goal area to take the throw and the resulting attack was one of the greatest moments of football history. The ball was won back by QPR but then quickly given away to Sergio Aguero. The Argentinean striker and prolific goalscorer took the ball and passed to Italian striker Mario Balliotelli. Mario was brought to the ground by a tackle but managed to stretch out his leg and poke the ball back to Aguero, who skilfully evaded a tackle in the box and blasted the ball into the back of the net. He screamed with joy as he had just put City back into the lead and back to the top of the table with mere seconds left on the clock. The news had already spead to the QPR players that they were also safe, and although it could have been much worse for them, they were happy to be playing the following season in the Premier League. They blasted the ball once again into City's half and just passed it around until the final whistle less than a minute later. Former Barcelona player and manager Pep Guardiola had just led Manchester City to their first league title since 1968 and they weren't going to let their rivals Manchester United forget it. Since then, success has belonged to Pep and his Sky Blues, who've won a cabinet full of trophies and created some incredible memories for fans. And it all started in this game.

5

FOOTBALL FUN FACTS

Here is a collection of fun football facts you can share with your family or friends at school or just to learn for yourself, as I used to love doing long ago - and still do!

1. The first-ever recorded football match took place in 1863 between two English teams, Barnes and Richmond.
2. The highest-scoring football match in history occurred in 2002, when Madagascar's AS Adema defeated SO l'Emyrne 149-0 after the opposing team deliberately scored own goals in protest.
3. The fastest goal in a World Cup match was scored by Hakan Şükür of Turkey, just 11 seconds into a game against South Korea in 2002.
4. The longest football match ever recorded lasted for three days and took place in 1965 between English teams Stockport County and Doncaster Rovers.
5. The oldest football club in the world is Sheffield FC, founded in 1857 in England.
6. Brazil holds the record for the most FIFA World Cup victories, with a total of five titles.

7. The largest football stadium in the world is the Rungrado 1st of May Stadium in Pyongyang, North Korea, with a seating capacity of 114,000.

8. The most goals scored by a single player in a calendar year is 91, achieved by Lionel Messi in 2012.

9. The fastest hat-trick in a professional football match was scored by Tommy Ross of Ross County in just 90 seconds in 1964.

10. The record for the most goals scored by a team in a single season of a major European league is held by Bayern Munich, who scored 101 goals in the 1971/72 Bundesliga season.

11. The most expensive football transfer in history (as of this writing) was Neymar's move from Barcelona to Paris Saint-Germain in 2017 for a fee of 222 million pounds.

12. The first player to score in every minute of a football match was Bafétimbi Gomis, who achieved this feat in a game between Lyon and Dinamo Zagreb in 2011.

13. The fastest recorded shot in football history was by Ronny Heberson, who registered a shot speed of 211 km/h (131 mph) in 2006.

14. The largest victory in an international football match was Australia's 31-0 win over American Samoa in 2001 during a World Cup qualifying match.

15. The fastest player in the history of football, as measured by official game data, is Arjen Robben, who reached a top speed of 37 km/h (23 mph).

16. The only player to have won the UEFA Champions League with three different clubs is Clarence Seedorf (Ajax, Real Madrid, and AC Milan).

17. Yaya Touré, an Ivorian midfielder, played a vital role in Manchester City's success in the English Premier League, helping the team win multiple titles. He was also a four-time African Player of the Year (2011-2014).

18. Abedi Pele from Ghana, known as the "Maestro," was a skilful attacking midfielder who played for Marseille and won the UEFA Champions League in 1993.

19. The youngest player to ever appear in a World Cup match is Norman Whiteside of Northern Ireland, who was 17 years and 41 days old when he played in the 1982 tournament.

20. The fastest hat-trick in the English Premier League was scored by Sadio Mané of Liverpool in just two minutes and 56 seconds in 2015.

21. The most goals scored by a player in a single World Cup tournament is 13, achieved by Just Fontaine of France in 1958.

22. The first football match to be broadcast on television was between Arsenal and Arsenal Reserves in 1937.

23. The most expensive goalkeeper transfer in history is Kepa Arrizabalaga's move in 2018 from Athletic Club to Chelsea for a fee of 80 million pounds.

24. The record for the most consecutive clean sheets in the English Premier League is held by Edwin van der Sar, who went 14 matches without conceding a goal for Manchester United in 2008-2009.

25. The first player to score 50 goals in a single season in Europe's top five leagues was Lionel Messi in the 2011/12 season.

26. The most expensive African player transfer is Wesley Fofana's move from Liecester City to Chelsea in 2022 for a fee of 80.4 million pounds.

27. The record for the most goals scored in a single European club competition season is 17, achieved by Cristiano Ronaldo in the 2013-2014 UEFA Champions League.

28. The largest margin of victory in a World Cup final is 4-0, which has occurred on three occasions: in 1954, 1970, and 1994.

29. The fastest red card in a World Cup match was shown to Uruguay's José Batista just 56 seconds into a game against Scotland in 1986.
30. The most successful club in the history of the English Premier League is Manchester United, with 13 titles.
31. The record for the most goals scored in a single season of the English Premier League is 36, achieved by Earling Haaland for Manchester City in the 2022-2023 season.
32. The most goals scored by an individual in a single calendar year is 91, achieved by Lionel Messi in 2012.
33. The highest attendance for a football match was recorded in 1950 in a game between Brazil and Uruguay at the Maracanã Stadium in Rio de Janeiro, with an estimated crowd of 199,854 spectators.
34. The most goals scored by a player in a single European club competition match is five, achieved by Lionel Messi for Barcelona against Bayer Leverkusen in 2012.
35. The fastest player to reach 100 Premier League goals is Alan Shearer, who accomplished this feat in 124 appearances for Blackburn Rovers and Newcastle United.
36. The record for the most goals scored by a team in a single English Premier League season is 106, achieved by Manchester City in the 2017/18 season.
37. The oldest outfield player to appear in a professional football match is Kazuyoshi Miura of Japan, who played for Yokohama FC at the age of 53 years and 210 days in 2021.
38. The most goals scored by a team in a single UEFA Champions League season is 45, achieved by Barcelona in the 1999-2000 campaign.
39. The first player to reach 100 goals in the UEFA Champions League is Cristiano Ronaldo, who achieved this milestone in 137 appearances. Lionel Messi is the fastest to reach 100, doing it in 123 games.

40. George Weah from Liberia became the first and, so far, the only African player to win the FIFA World Player of the Year award (now known as the FIFA Ballon d'Or) in 1995.

41. The most consecutive league titles won by a team is nine, achieved by Celtic FC in Scotland from 1965 to 1974.

42. The most goals scored by a team in a single FIFA World Cup tournament is 27, achieved by Hungary in 1954.

43. The youngest player to score a goal in the UEFA Champions League is Ansu Fati of Barcelona, who achieved this at the age of 17 years and 40 days in 2019.

44. The fastest player to reach 100 goals in Serie A is Andriy Shevchenko, who accomplished this in 143 appearances.

45. The most goals scored by a team in a single La Liga season is 121, achieved by Barcelona in the 2011-2012 campaign.

46. The oldest player to appear in a FIFA World Cup match is Essam El-Hadary of Egypt, who played at the age of 45 years and 161 days in 2018.

47. Ryan Giggs is the only Premier League player to have scored 100 competition goals without scoring a hat-trick.

48. Steven Gerrard swapped shirts with over 100 players throughout his career, but never with a player from arch rivals Manchester United.

49. The most goals scored by a team in a single UEFA European Championship tournament is 13, achieved by France in 1984.

50. There are 869 days between Messi and Ronaldo's birth dates, which is precisely the same number of days between their sons' birth dates.

51. The highest-scoring draw in a World Cup match is 4-4, which has occurred on two occasions: Austria vs. Switzerland in 1954 and Hungary vs. Uruguay in 1954.

52. The most goals scored by an individual in a single UEFA European Championship tournament is nine, achieved by Michel Platini of France in 1984.

53. Zinedine Zidane was never caught offside throughout his entire playing career.

54. The most goals scored by a team in a single FIFA Club World Cup tournament is eight, achieved by Barcelona in 2011.

55. The youngest player to score a hat-trick in the English Premier League is Robbie Fowler, who achieved this at the age of 18 years and 335 days in 1994.

56. The fastest player to reach 100 goals in Serie A is Andriy Shevchenko, who accomplished this in 143 appearances.

57. Major League Soccer (MLS) is the top professional soccer league in the United States. It was established in 1993 and has grown in popularity and competitiveness over the years.

58. The United States hosted the FIFA World Cup in 1994, which helped boost the sport's popularity in the country.

59. The US Women's National Team (USWNT) is one of the most successful women's soccer teams in the world, having won the FIFA Women's World Cup four times (1991, 1999, 2015, and 2019).

60. The popularity of soccer among youth in the USA has been steadily increasing. It is one of the most-played sports by children and teenagers.

61. The US Men's National Team (USMNT) has made several appearances in the FIFA World Cup and has had notable successes, including reaching the quarterfinals in 2002.

62. Soccer is the fourth most-watched sport among American television viewers, after American football, basketball, and baseball.

63. The growth of soccer in the USA can be seen through the establishment of soccer-specific stadiums for MLS teams,

providing dedicated venues for matches and enhancing the overall fan experience.

64. Kalusha Bwalya from Zambia is a respected figure in African football. He was named African Footballer of the Year in 1988 and had a successful international career, representing Zambia in multiple Africa Cup of Nations tournaments.

65. The U.S. soccer pyramid includes multiple tiers of professional and semi-professional leagues, providing opportunities for players to develop and progress in their careers.

66. Soccer participation at the grassroots level is widespread in the USA, with numerous youth clubs, recreational leagues, and school programs promoting the sport and nurturing young talent.

67. Samuel Eto'o from Cameroon is considered one of the greatest African players of all time. He won the African Player of the Year award a record four times (2003, 2004, 2005, and 2010).

68. Roger Milla from Cameroon made history as the oldest goal scorer in FIFA World Cup history during the 1994 tournament at the age of 42. He also played a key role in Cameroon's memorable run to the quarterfinals in the 1990 World Cup.

69. Major League Soccer has expanded significantly since its inception, with new teams being added over the years. The league now consists of 27 teams, with plans for further expansion.

70. The only goalkeeper to win the Ballon d'Or, awarded to the best player in the world, is Lev Yashin of the Soviet Union in 1963.

71. The UEFA Champions League is the most prestigious club football competition in Europe. It was first held in the 1955-1956 season and involves the top teams from

various European leagues competing for the title. Real Madrid holds the record for the most Champions League titles, having won it 13 times.

72. UEFA European Championship, commonly referred to as the Euro, is the premier national team football tournament in Europe. It takes place every four years and features teams from across the continent competing for the title. The most successful teams in Euro history are Germany and Spain, with three titles each.

73. The Ballon d'Or is an annual football award presented by *France Football* magazine. It is awarded to the best male football player in the world. European players have dominated the Ballon d'Or, with Lionel Messi and Cristiano Ronaldo winning it multiple times in recent years.

74. The match between Spanish football clubs Barcelona and Real Madrid is known as El Clásico. It is one of the biggest rivalries in football, showcasing intense competition between two of the most successful clubs in the sport. The matches between Barcelona and Real Madrid often attract global attention and have a rich history of memorable encounters.

75. The European Golden Shoe is an award given to the top goal scorer across European leagues in a single season. The award takes into account the strength of each league, with goals scored in more competitive leagues receiving higher points. Notable recipients of the European Golden Shoe include Lionel Messi, Cristiano Ronaldo, and Luis Suárez.

76. The Football Association, commonly known as the FA, is the governing body for football in England. It was founded on October 26, 1863, making it the oldest football association in the world.

77. The FA is responsible for establishing and maintaining the Laws of the Game, which are the rules that govern football worldwide. The Laws of the Game are regularly updated and modified by the International Football Association Board (IFAB), of which the FA is a member.

78. The FA is the owner of Wembley Stadium, one of the most iconic football stadiums in the world. Located in London, Wembley Stadium has a seating capacity of over 90,000 and is the home venue for the England national team.

79. The FA Cup is the oldest domestic football competition in the world. The tournament is organized by the FA and involves teams from various levels of English football competing for the trophy. The FA Cup final, held at Wembley Stadium, is one of the most prestigious matches in English football.

80. The FA is responsible for overseeing the England national football team. It selects the national team manager, organizes international fixtures, and supports the development of football at all levels in England, including grassroots initiatives and youth development programs.

81. South America has a rich footballing history, and the sport's roots in the region can be traced back to the late 19th century. British merchants and workers introduced football to countries like Argentina and Uruguay, where it quickly gained popularity.

82. The Copa America is the oldest international football tournament in the world. It was first held in 1916 and has since become the premier competition for national teams in South America. The tournament has seen fierce rivalries and memorable matches, showcasing the talent and passion of South American football.

83. The term "Maracanazo" refers to the unexpected victory of Uruguay over Brazil in the 1950 FIFA World Cup final held at the Maracanã Stadium in Rio de Janeiro, Brazil.

Uruguay's 2-1 win in front of a massive crowd is considered one of the greatest upsets in football history.

84. South America has produced some of the greatest footballers of all time. Two legendary figures who represent the region's footballing pedigree are Pelé from Brazil and Diego Maradona from Argentina. They achieved immense success on the international stage and became global icons of the sport.

85. South American teams have enjoyed remarkable success in international competitions. Brazil is the most successful national team, having won the FIFA World Cup a record five times. Argentina, Uruguay, and other South American nations have also had significant achievements, making the region a powerhouse in world football.

86. Goal-line technology was introduced to eliminate controversial goal decisions. It uses multiple cameras to track the ball's position and determine if it has crossed the goal line. The system provides instant feedback to the referee, ensuring accurate goal decisions.

87. VAR is a system that allows referees to review decisions using video replays. It helps in making more accurate judgements regarding goals, penalties, red cards, and cases of mistaken identity. VAR has been implemented in various leagues and tournaments around the world, including major international competitions.

88. Hawk-Eye technology is widely used in football to assist with offside decisions. It utilizes multiple high-speed cameras to track the movement of players and determine their positioning accurately. Hawk-Eye provides real-time information to the officials, aiding them in making correct offside judgements.

89. Players now have access to various wearable technologies to monitor their performance and fitness levels. GPS tracking devices, heart rate monitors, and

other sensors are integrated into kits to gather data on players' physical exertion, distance covered, and other metrics. This data helps coaches and sports scientists optimize training regimes and enhance player performance.

90. Virtual reality technology has made its way into football training. Players can use VR headsets to simulate match scenarios and practise their skills in a virtual environment. This immersive training approach allows players to enhance decision-making, spatial awareness, and reaction times in a realistic and controlled setting.

91. The origins of football can be traced back to various ancient civilizations. Games involving kicking a ball were played in China, Egypt, Greece, and Rome, among other places. These early forms of football often had different rules and variations, but they all involved the basic concept of using the feet to propel a ball.

92. The modern codification of football began in the 19th century. The Football Association (FA) in England was established in 1863 and played a significant role in standardizing the rules of the game. The FA's rulebook became the basis for the Laws of the Game, which are still followed today.

93. The inaugural FIFA World Cup took place in 1930 in Uruguay. Thirteen teams participated in the tournament, with Uruguay emerging as the champions. The World Cup has since become the most prestigious international football tournament, held every four years and capturing the attention of millions of fans worldwide.

94. And finally, football has grown to become the most popular sport globally. It is played and followed by billions of people across all continents. Major international competitions like the FIFA World Cup and regional tournaments such as the UEFA Champions

League and Copa America attract massive audiences and generate immense excitement and passion.

No matter where you tune in for your first match, if you're anything like me you will be instantly hooked on this exhilarating rollercoaster of a sport we call 'the beautiful game' and want to know more and more. Hopefully this book has taught you some facts so you can impress your friends with your new knowledge of stats, players, positions, rules and some of the greatest moments of the greatest sport in the world. Football.